Microsoft® Excel for Accounting

THE FIRST COURSE

Katherine T. Smith, D.B.A.
Business Consultant

L. Murphy Smith, D.B.A., CPA
Texas A&M University

Lawrence C. Smith, Jr., Ph.D.
Louisiana Tech University

Prentice Hall

UPPER SADDLE RIVER, NEW JERSEY 07458

Acquisitions Editor: Alana Bradley
Editor-in-Chief: P. J. Boardman
Editorial Assistant: Jane Avery
Executive Marketing Manager: Beth Toland
Managing Editor (Production): John Roberts
Permissions Coordinator: Suzanne Grappi
Associate Director, Manufacturing: Vincent Scelta
Production Manager: Arnold Vila
Manufacturing Buyer: Michelle Klein
Design Manager: Patricia Smythe
Cover Design: Kiwi Design
Printer/Binder: Victor Graphics

Pearson Education LTD.
Pearson Education Australia PTY, Limited
Pearson Education Singapore, Pte. Ltd
Pearson Education North Asia Ltd
Pearson Education, Canada, Ltd
Pearson Educación de Mexico, S.A. de C.V.
Pearson Education–Japan
Pearson Education Malaysia, Pte. Ltd

10 9 8
ISBN 0-13-008551-0

DEDICATION

To the students who use this book. We hope each of you will enjoy the true success which is measured by moral character and personal integrity. "A good name is more desirable than great riches; to be esteemed is better than silver or gold" (Proverbs 22:1).

To our children: Hannah, Jacob, and Tracy. "Children are a gift from God; they are His reward" (Psalm 127:3).

To our parents: Genita and Hubert Taken, and Doris and Junior Smith.

KTS & LMS

To Doris Elaine Barfoot Smith, my beautiful wife. "A worthy wife is her husband's joy and crown" (Proverbs 12:4).

To the memory of D. Gray Miley, the consummate professor.

LCS

CONTENTS

v

PREFACE

The purpose of this book is to introduce students to the fundamental tools and techniques available in Microsoft Excel™ spreadsheet software. Applications are presented that pertain to specific financial accounting and principles topics. Students will learn through experience by following directions and creating the example worksheets shown in each chapter. Assignments may be selected from those contained within the book or other sources provided by your instructor.

The book provides detailed instructions for using Microsoft Excel. These instructions are designed for the most current version of Excel but are applicable for most other versions as well. Additional information is available on the website corresponding to this book.

WEBSITE

For updates, example files, suggested assignment schedules, and other helpful information, check the website (http://www.IOLBV.com/murphy/EXCEL4ACCT1).

ACKNOWLEDGMENTS

The authors are grateful for the contributions to this project made by Paul Ashcroft, Rod Banister, Alana Bradley, and Kristi Shuey. Additionally, the authors appreciate the support and encouragement they have received, over the years, from Natalie Allen, Nancy Cassidy, Dot Davis, Patricia Hayes, Danny and Susan Ivancevich, Larry Joiner, David Kerr, Stan Kratchman, Jeff Miller, Steve McDuffie, Chris Osborne, Steve Salter, Jim Sena, Mary Stasny, Bob Strawser, and Jim Thompson.

About the Authors

Katherine Taken Smith

Dr. Katherine T. Smith has served on the faculties at the University of Mississippi and Louisiana Tech University. Dr. Smith has authored numerous research articles which have appeared in various professional journals such as *The CPA Journal, Today's CPA, Accounting Education* (UK), and *National Public Accountant*. Currently she serves on the editorial boards of five national journals. She has authored five books, including an educational novel entitled *The Bottom Line is Betrayal* (http://www.iolbv.com/murphy/novels/) which has been described as an "instructional thriller" that provides an innovative way to present business concepts and issues to students. In addition, she has made presentations at professional meetings in the U.S. and abroad.

L. Murphy Smith

Dr. L. Murphy Smith, CPA is Assistant Department Head and Professor in the Accounting Department at Texas A&M University. He received his doctorate from Louisiana Tech University. Dr. Smith's accomplishments include numerous professional journal articles, research grants, books, and professional meeting presentations in the U.S. and abroad. His major research interests are systems, auditing, ethics, and international issues. His work has been cited in various news media, including *Fortune, USA Today*, and *The Wall Street Journal*. Among the books he has published, his accounting information systems text (http://acct.tamu.edu/smith/books/aisbook/) is now in its third edition. He serves on the editorial boards of several journals, including *Advances in International Accounting, Journal of Information Systems, Research on Accounting Ethics, Teaching Business Ethics*, and *The CPA Journal*.

Lawrence C. Smith, Jr.

Lawrence C. Smith, Jr., PhD is a Professor of Economics at Louisiana Tech University. He received his doctorate from the University of Mississippi. He has developed expertise on a wide variety of business and economics issues. In his distinguished career, Dr. Smith has made significant academic contributions in teaching, research, and service. He has played many roles in various professional organizations, including serving 27 years as Secretary-Treasurer of the Academy of Economics and Finance. In 1999 he was selected as the first Fellow of the Academy of Economics and Finance.

Dr. Smith's accomplishments include numerous professional journal articles, books, and professional meeting presentations. Among the journals in which he has published are the following: *Journal of Economic Education, Journal of Economics and Finance, Southwestern Economic Review, Journal of Real Estate Appraisal and Economics*, and *Oil, Gas & Energy Quarterly*.

Computer Basics 1

This chapter briefly describes components of the personal computer, operating systems software, Windows, and starting your spreadsheet program.

COMPONENTS OF THE COMPUTER

As shown in Exhibit 1.1, the basic personal computer system consists of a monitor, keyboard, and a central processing unit (CPU). The CPU consists of three components: main memory, arithmetic logic unit, and supervisory control. Main memory includes random access memory (RAM) and read-only memory (ROM). The RAM of a typical personal computer may be as little as 640 kilobytes (K) or as much as 256 megabytes (MB).

The box or chassis containing the CPU also contains other devices such as the graphics card which connects to the monitor, a parallel port which connects to a printer, a serial port which connects to a mouse, a modem which connects to the phone line, a hard disk drive which provides secondary storage (typically ranging from four to 100 gigabytes), a floppy disk drive, and a CD-ROM or CD-RW drive. Another increasingly common feature on personal computers is a network card (e.g. ethernet) which enables a computer to be connected to a local area network or intranet, which then permits access to the Internet and the World Wide Web. The most widely used floppy disk drive is the 3.5 inch high density (HD) drive. The 3.5 inch HD disk can store 1.44 megabytes (MB) of data. A CD-ROM or CD-RW can store up to 640 MB of data.

The keyboard on your computer is made up of three basic sections: the function keys, the numeric key pad, and the alphanumeric keys. The alphanumeric keys, the main part of the keyboard, include letters, numbers, and a variety of symbols. The function keys, labeled F1 through F12, have different uses depending on the software currently in use.

The numeric pad is located on the right side of your keyboard. A significant key on the numeric pad is the NUM LOCK key, which is a toggle key that enables the user to switch between the number keys and the cursor control keys located on the numeric pad.

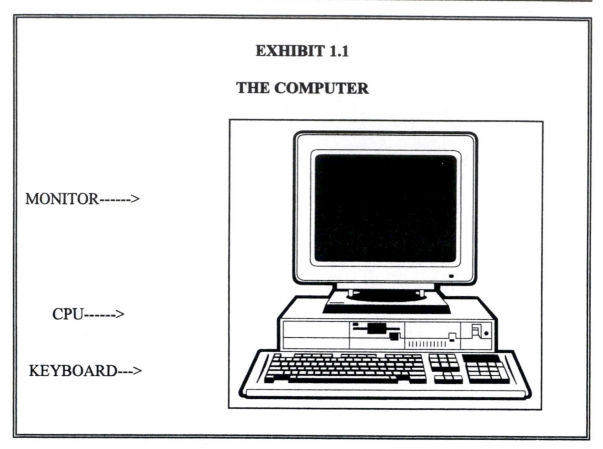

EXHIBIT 1.1

THE COMPUTER

MONITOR------>

CPU------>

KEYBOARD--->

OPERATING SYSTEMS SOFTWARE

An operating system runs your computer and manages your computer's activities. The operating system of the personal computer functions much like the operating systems on the mainframe or minicomputer. For the IBM-compatible system, the most popular operating system is Microsoft's Windows. The Apple Macintosh has an operating system called System 7.

Windows is a set of software programs that provides a graphical user interface. When running Windows, the computer user interacts with the computer visually and by use of a mouse rather than typing commands. New versions of Windows are typically released with much fanfare. Windows XP was introduced in New York City to a backdrop of a gospel choir singing "America the Beautiful," followed by popstar Sting performing a free concert in Bryant Park.

WINDOWS OPERATING SYSTEM

The most prominent feature of Windows is the use of icons (little pictures) to represent programs or groups of programs. After Windows is loaded (running), you run programs such as Excel by moving the pointer to the icon and double-clicking the left mouse button. A program icon represents a "shortcut" in Windows. Programs can also be accessed via the "start" button on the lower menu-bar. By clicking on "Start," you are given various options such as Run, Find, Settings, and Programs.

Microsoft periodically upgrades its Windows program. The current release is Windows XP. In Windows, "folders" and "shortcuts" refer to directories and executable programs. A folder may contain several shortcuts (which access specific programs such as Excel or Lotus 1-2-3). Each folder has a menu bar which allows creation of shortcuts or folders within that folder (select "File"-"New").

LOADING YOUR EXCEL SPREADSHEET PROGRAM

Excel by Microsoft Corporation is the most widely used spreadsheet software. In order to start Excel, follow these steps:

1.   In Windows, use your mouse to click on the "Start" button on the bottom left side of your computer screen. The button should expand into a box with several options for selection.

2.   From the Start menu, select the Programs options, which will open another box with options. If Microsoft Excel is listed separately, double-click the Excel option to open (run) the program. If there is not a separate listing for Microsoft Excel, then scroll to the Microsoft Office option and select Microsoft Excel.

OR

*   If an Excel icon is shown on screen, simply double-click on that icon.

BASIC COMMANDS

SAVING A FILE

A worksheet is saved like any other file by using the following commands:

1.   Choose "File" in the menu bar and select the Save-As option.
2.   The Save-As menu box will appear and the name "Book1.xls" will be highlighted in the file name box. "Book1" is simply the default name which Excel uses and "xls" is the filename extension of an Excel worksheet. You can replace "Book1" with a new filename; we recommend keeping the "xls" extension so that your file will be recognized as an Excel worksheet.
3.   Now that you have named the worksheet, you can save it in the future by simply clicking on the Save icon (picture of a floppy disk).

CLOSING FILES

Similar to other files, a worksheet is closed by simply clicking on the "X" button in the upper right-hand corner of the menu bar on your worksheet.

RETRIEVING FILES

A worksheet is retrieved like any file by using the following commands:

1.   Click on the "Open" icon (picture of an open folder).
2.   An Open File box will appear with a list of files or folders. Double-click on the file you want opened. Note: If the file is not listed, then you are in the wrong folder. Access the correct folder by clicking on the arrow next to the "Looking in" box at the top. A list of folders or directories will appear for your choosing. Alternatively, you can search for a file with Windows Explorer program (using "Tools - Find").

EXITING

The Excel program can be exited like any other program by clicking on the "X" button in the upper right-hand corner of the screen (this appears above the "X" button used for closing the worksheet).

Making a Worksheet 2

WORKSHEET LAYOUT

Once the spreadsheet software is loaded, a screen appears similar to Exhibit 2.1. A spreadsheet file is often referred to as a worksheet.

EXHIBIT 2.1
BASIC EXCEL WORKSHEET

The letters across the top of a worksheet correspond to columns. The numbers along the left side of a worksheet correspond to rows. The box at the intersection of a column and row is referred to as the cell location. Cells are where data, either text or mathematical expressions, are entered. In Exhibit 2.1, the words "Cell A1" have been typed into cell A1. Directly above the cell is the control panel which shows the cell designation, in this case it is A1. To the right of that, next to an equal sign, you'll notice another panel containing "Cell A1." When a cell is clicked upon, its contents automatically appear in this panel.

Each Excel file, called a workbook, can hold several worksheets. Worksheets are saved, closed and printed like any other file, by clicking on the "File" selection in the top menu bar or by clicking on the appropriate icons.

AN ILLUSTRATION

To begin your familiarization with Excel worksheets, we will create a worksheet using just the essential commands. Step-by-step instructions to accomplish these commands will be provided.

Assume that you work in the accounting department at a local grocery store. Your boss has requested a breakdown of sales by department, comparing the last two years. To accomplish this, we'll create a worksheet with the data contained in the example worksheet shown in Exhibit 2.2. To begin, click on cell A1 with your mouse and type in "Sales." When finished typing, press Enter or click on another cell; the typed data will automatically be inserted into the worksheet. Now click on cell A3 and type in "Produce." Another way to move among the cells is to use the arrow keys. Proceed to type in the remaining data so that your worksheet looks like Exhibit 2.2. Column B is left empty simply for the purpose of improving the appearance of the worksheet.

EXHIBIT 2.2
GROCERY STORE WORKSHEET

	A	B	C	D	E
1	Sales				
2			12/31/x1	12/31/x2	
3	Produce		300	350	
4	Bakery		100	150	
5	Florist		50	20	
6	Deli		225	290	
7	Meat		550	600	
8	Dairy		410	500	
9					
10					

Note that Excel automatically right-justifies a number after it is entered into a cell. If you make a mistake in typing the numbers, the ensuing section on editing will reveal how to correct it.

EDITING

A cell can be put into edit mode by double clicking on the cell. Excel will then allow you to move around within the cell and change the contents. If you want to replace the entire contents of a cell, simply click on the cell once and type in the new contents. If you want to delete the entire contents of a cell, click on the cell and press the delete key.

As noted earlier, when a cell is clicked upon, its contents automatically enter the panel at the top of the worksheet next to the equal sign (=). Another way to edit a cell is to place your cursor within this panel and type.

If you make a mistake using any of the following commands, you can undo it by clicking on the "undo" icon (an arrow curving backwards).

MOVING CELL CONTENTS

Perhaps our worksheet would look better if "Sales" was placed more in the center of the worksheet. To move "Sales" to cell C1:

1. Click on the cell you wish to move (A1).
2. Position your cursor anywhere along the border of the cell until the cursor turns into a white arrow. Hold down the left mouse button and drag the arrow to the new cell. Release the mouse button, and the contents will appear in the new cell.

To move a block of cells, highlight the cells by holding down the left mouse button and then move the entire block at once. Cells can also be moved by using the "copy and paste" commands (discussed later in the chapter).

INSERTING ROWS AND COLUMNS

Suppose you decide that the worksheet would look better with a space between the title and the date headings. You want to insert a blank row between "Sales" on row 1 and the dates on row 2. The row can be inserted as follows:

1. Rows are added **above** the cell pointer, so position your cell pointer accordingly. In our example, click on any cell in row 2.
2. Click on "Insert" in the menu bar and choose "Rows" to insert.

Suppose you want to insert a column between the years (columns C and D). Columns are added to the **left** of the pointer, so to add the column in our example, click on any cell in column D. Click on "Insert" in the menu bar and choose "Columns." Exhibit 2.3 shows the new format with a blank row 2 and the sales figures in columns C and E.

EXHIBIT 2.3
GROCERY STORE WORKSHEET

	A	B	C	D	E
1			Sales		
2					
3			12/31/x1		12/31/x2
4	Produce		300		350
5	Bakery		100		150
6	Florist		50		20
7	Deli		225		290
8	Meat		550		600
9	Dairy		410		500
10					
11					

DELETING AND SHIFTING CELLS

Assume that the Florist department was discontinued at our store last month and should not be in the worksheet. As previously discussed, the contents of a cell can be removed by clicking on the cell and pressing the delete key. However, we want the florist data removed without leaving a row of empty cells. This is accomplished by deleting the unwanted row and shifting the remaining rows up. In regards to our grocery store worksheet, use the following commands:

1. Click on the cell which contains "Florist."
2. Click on "Edit" in the menu bar and choose the Delete option.
3. Excel gives you the option of deleting the entire row, click on that option. The rows below the deleted row will be shifted up.

If we had not chosen the option of deleting the entire row, than only the cell containing "florist" would have been deleted and only the cells within column A would have been shifted up. If an entire column is deleted, columns will be shifted to the left.

CENTERING

Data within a single cell can be centered by clicking on the cell and then clicking on the icon which displays centered lines. The icon is found on the top toolbar, just to the right of the bold (**B**), italicize (*I*), and underline (U) icons. Center each of the dates in the worksheet. Multiple cells may be centered at the same time by first highlighting the range of cells and then clicking on the icon.

Suppose we need a different heading on the worksheet. Delete "Sales." In the same cell, type "Grocery Store Sales by Department." The heading will run over into the adjacent empty cells. Press enter to leave the edit mode. To center the new heading between columns A and E, first highlight row 1 from A to E. Then click on the icon with the boxed in "a" (merge and center icon). Exhibit 2.4 shows the new heading.

CHANGING COLUMN OR ROW WIDTH

When the spreadsheet program is first loaded, the column width will be eight characters. If your cell data exceeds the cell width, the data will simply run into the adjacent empty cell. However, if the adjacent cell is not empty, the overflow data will be truncated at the cell border. To avoid this, column width can be changed. Using our example worksheet, type the heading "Total Sales Per Year" into cell A9. To accommodate the long heading, widen column A using the following instructions. Note: It is best to be out of the edit mode when changing cell width; click on a blank cell to exit the edit mode.

1. Position the cursor at the top of the screen on the mid-point between the lettered column headings (i.e., between A and B). The cursor should change into a "+."
2. Click-and-drag using the left mouse key; hold it while "dragging" the column to a different width.

Your worksheet should now resemble Exhibit 2.4. (We will total the sales per year in Chapter 3 using a special Excel command.) Row width can be changed by positioning the cursor between the row numbers on the left side of the worksheet.

COPY AND PASTE

The "copy and paste" commands enable you to duplicate the contents of one or more cells to other locations on the worksheet. Anything already in the receiving cell will be deleted. To copy and paste, highlight the cell(s) and then click on the copy and paste icons. If you want to delete the cell contents from the original location, you can use the cut and paste icons or the commands which are accessed via "Edit" on the menu bar.

EXHIBIT 2.4
GROCERY STORE WORKSHEET

	A	B	C	D	E
1	Grocery Store Sales by Department				
2					
3			12/31/x1		12/31/x2
4	Produce		300		350
5	Bakery		100		150
6	Deli		225		290
7	Meat		550		600
8	Dairy		410		500
9	Total Sales Per Year				
10					
11					

Special paste commands can be accessed by clicking on "Edit" in the menu bar and choosing the "Paste Special" option. Here are two useful "paste special" commands which can be used on cells or entire worksheets.

1. The "Microsoft Excel Worksheet" option allows you to paste a worksheet into a document (e.g. a Word file) and then activate Excel by simply clicking on the worksheet in your document.

2. The "Picture" option pastes the worksheet contents without the gridlines. The grocery store worksheet was pasted into Exhibit 2.5 using the Picture option.

EXHIBIT 2.5
WORKSHEET PASTED USING "PICTURE" OPTION

Grocery Store Sales by Department

	12/31/x1	12/31/x2
Produce	300	350
Bakery	100	150
Deli	225	290
Meat	550	600
Dairy	410	500
Total Sales Per Year		

PRINTING

For printing your worksheet, it is helpful to first highlight the section you want printed and then click on "File" in the menu bar. Select "Print." Under the print options, choose "Selection." Another very useful step is to select "File - Print Preview" to see how your output will look. By skipping these steps, and depending on where the cursor is, you could print several pages unnecessarily. Occasionally, you may need to designate the range of cells to be printed. To do so, highlight the range to be printed (e.g. A1 to H40) and then click on File - Print Area - Set Print Area.

Formulas, Functions, and Formatting 3

This chapter presents Excel features which are especially useful for manipulating numbers within accounting related worksheets. The features include automatic sums, formulas, functions, and numeric formatting.

The Grocery Store worksheet that was created in Chapter 2 will also be used in this chapter as an example. If you do not still have the worksheet on your computer, recreate it as shown in Exhibit 3.1

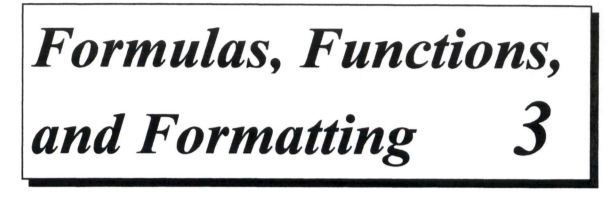

EXHIBIT 3.1
GROCERY STORE WORKSHEET

	A	B	C	D	E
1	Grocery Store Sales by Department				
2					
3			12/31/x1		12/31/x2
4	Bakery		100		150
5	Deli		225		290
6	Produce		300		350
7	Dairy		410		500
8	Meat		550		600
9	Total Sales Per Year				
10					

AUTOMATIC SUMS

Excel contains an icon with the Greek sigma sign (Σ). This icon is called "Autosum" and will automatically sum numbers within the cells you select. Using the example worksheet, total each year's sales using the following instructions:

1.   Highlight the cells to be summed (for year 1: cells C4 through C8).

2.   Click on the Autosum button. The total will automatically be inserted into the next cell.

In the latest version of Excel, the Autosum icon is accompanied by a down arrow. Upon clicking on the arrow, other functions will be displayed, such as averaging numbers and counting cells.

Note: If a number has more characters than a cell will hold, the number signs (####) will appear. To correct this, simply widen the column.

Repeat the Autosum process for the second year's column. To enhance the appearance of the worksheet, place a line under the figures being summed (i.e., cells C8 and E8). To place an underscore in a cell, click on the appropriate cell and then click on the underscore icon (U). Your worksheet should now resemble Exhibit 3.2.

EXHIBIT 3.2
GROCERY STORE WORKSHEET

	A	B	C	D	E
1	Grocery Store Sales by Department				
2					
3			12/31/x1		12/31/x2
4	Bakery		100		150
5	Deli		225		290
6	Produce		300		350
7	Dairy		410		500
8	Meat		550		600
9	Total Sales Per Year		1585		1890

FORMULAS

WRITING FORMULAS

Formulas can be used to manipulate numeric data. They are entered just as they would be processed algebraically. For example, to add the contents of cells C9 and E9, the following steps are necessary:

1.   In the cell in which you want the result to appear, type the formula: =C9+E9

2.   Press "Enter" to place the results of the equation in the cell.

The same process applies to subtraction, division, and multiplication. The multiplication symbol is the asterisk (*). The division symbol is the slash (/).

Note: When an equal sign is the very first thing entered, Excel knows it is a mathematical expression. If there is a space before the equal sign, Excel will read it as text.

COPYING FORMULAS

We will use our grocery store worksheet to practice writing and copying formulas. Suppose the boss wants a column which shows how much sales have increased or decreased between the two years. Type the heading "Difference" into cell D3. Next, in cell D4, type the formula: =E4-C4. Press "Enter."

Instead of entering the formula into multiple cells, you can copy this formula into the other cells. The cell addresses will automatically adjust as you copy a formula from one cell to another. If a formula is copied down the length of a column, the address will change corresponding to the row in which the formula is placed. Copy the formula into the other cells in your worksheet by:

1.   Click on the cell which contains the formula (D4). Put the cursor on the small box in the bottom right corner of the cell (the fill handle); the cursor will turn to a "+".

2.   Drag the cell over the range of cells you want to fill (D5 through D9).

When the formula was copied into cell D5, the formula automatically changed from "=E4-C4" to "=E5-C5." This is referred to as **relative addressing**. Relative addressing occurs for both rows and columns.

Your worksheet should now resemble Exhibit 3.3. In the newest version of Excel, an Autofill options box pops up; it can be ignored. Autofill will be discussed in Chapter 5.

The alternative to relative addressing is called **absolute addressing**. This means that the cell references do not adjust, but they remain exactly as they were in the source cell of the copy procedure. To make a formula absolute you must precede that portion of the formula with a dollar sign ($). Thus, if you want to copy a formula such as =C2*D5 and you want to make C2 an absolute address, you would type the formula as =C2*D5 before copying.

EXHIBIT 3.3
GROCERY STORE WORKSHEET

	A	B	C	D	E
1		Grocery Store Sales by Department			
2					
3			12/31/x1	Difference	12/31/x2
4	Bakery		100	50	150
5	Deli		225	65	290
6	Produce		300	50	350
7	Dairy		410	90	500
8	Meat		550	50	600
9	Total Sales Per Year		1585	305	1890
10					

FUNCTIONS

Functions are basically pre-written formulas. They save time and increase accuracy. We will create a new worksheet to practice using functions. Remember that a workbook can contain several worksheets. If you want to add a new worksheet to an existing workbook file, simply click on the tab at the bottom entitled "Sheet2." If you prefer an new workbook file, one can be created by clicking on the icon of a blank white sheet of paper found on the upper-left of the tool bar.

Assume that you are asked to prepare a worksheet to calculate loan payments based on the information below. Type the data from Exhibit 3.4 into a new worksheet. Note that column A will need to be widened to accommodate the words "annual payment." Review: To widen a column, position the cursor on the mid-point between the lettered column headings. When the cursor changes into a "+," click-and-drag the column width.

EXHIBIT 3.4
LOAN PAYMENTS WORKSHEET

	A	B	C	D
1	Rate	0.1	0.05	0.06
2	Years	10	20	8
3	Principal	100000	30000	20000
4	Annual Payments			

To calculate the annual payments for our example loan payments worksheet, the use of the @PMT function is explained below.

1. Click on the cell in which you want the annual payment to appear (B4).
2. Click on the "fx" icon which represents the Functions Wizard.
3. Choose Financial under the Functions category box.
4. Choose PMT under the Function name box. Then click OK.
5. Enter the cell locations which contain the rate, nper, and pv. Use the mouse to click on the different boxes.
     In this example, rate is B1. Nper (years) is B2. Pv (principal) is B3. (The formula is =PMT(rate, nper, pv). Excel will also ask for fv and type; leave those blank. Click on OK.

Note: If a cell is not wide enough to accommodate a number, then you will see "######" in the cell. Simply widen the column and the correct number ($16,274.54) will appear. Excel automatically formats the loan payment in dollars.

Do not use the Functions Wizard to calculate the remaining annual payments, instead we will save time by copying the formula into the other cells. Review on how to copy a formula: Click on the cell which contains the formula (B4). Put the cursor on the small box in the bottom right corner of the cell; the cursor will turn to a "+". Drag the cell over the range of cells you want to fill (C4 and D4).

Exhibit 3.5 includes the annual loan payment calculations.

EXHIBIT 3.5
LOAN PAYMENTS WORKSHEET

	A	B	C	D
1	Rate	0.1	0.05	0.06
2	Years	10	20	8
3	Principal	100000	30000	20000
4	Annual Payment	($16,274.54)	($2,407.28)	($3,220.72)

DATE AND OTHER FUNCTIONS

The Functions Wizard of Excel has many useful functions available in addition to those that perform basic arithmetic. For example, by typing "=today( )" into a cell, the worksheet will always show the actual date. If you typed a particular date into the parenthesis, the worksheet would always show that date. Other functions and their symbols are described in Exhibit 3.6.

EXHIBIT 3.6
EXCEL FUNCTIONS

SYMBOL   DESCRIPTION

Financial Functions:

FV	Returns the future value of an investment.
IPMT	Returns the interest payment for an investment for a given period.
IRR	Returns the internal rate of return for a series of cash flows.
NPV	Returns the net present value of an investment based on a series of periodic cash flows and a discount rate.
PMT	Returns period payments for an annuity.
PV	Returns the present value of an investment.
RATE	Returns the interest rate per period of an annuity.

Date and Time Functions:

DATE	Returns the serial number of a particular date.
DAY	Converts a serial number to a particular day of the month.
DAYS360	Calculates the number of days between two dates based on a 360-day year.
TIMEVALUE	Converts the time in the form of text to a serial number.
TODAY	Returns the serial number of today's date.

Math and Trig Functions:

COUNTIF	Returns the number of nonblank cells in a given range which meet the given criteria.
INT	Rounds a number down to the nearest integer.
ROUND	Rounds a number to the specified number of digits.
SUBTOTAL	Returns a subtotal in a list or database.
SUM	Adds the specified numbers.

Statistical Functions:

AVERAGE	Returns the average of the specified numbers
COUNT	Counts how many numbers are in a given range.
MAX	Returns the maximum number in a specified range.
MEDIAN	Returns the median of the specified numbers.
MIN	Returns the minimum number in a specified range.
MODE	Returns the most common value in a specified range.

NUMERIC FORMATTING

Using our example loans payment worksheet, we will format the numbers in a simple manner using the tool bar icons. Customized formatting using the menu bar will also be discussed.

PERCENTAGE SYMBOL

The icon of a percentage symbol (%) automatically converts numbers to percentages. In your worksheet, select the cells which contain values for Rate (B1 through D1) and click on the percentage icon. If your software doesn't have the percentage icon, click on "Format - Cells" in the menu bar and then select "Number - Percentage." Exhibit 3.7 shows the percentages.

CURRENCY STYLE

The icon of a dollar sign ($) is called "currency style" and will automatically add a dollar sign, decimal, and cents places to any cell you select. In your worksheet, select the cells which contain values for Principal and click on the dollar icon. Alternatively, click on "Format - Cells" in the top menu bar and then select "Number - Currency."

If you accidentally insert a currency style into the wrong cell, you must go to the Format menu to un-format the cell. Click on "Format" in the menu bar and choose "Cells." Under the Number tab choose "Currency." Excel will offer several options, scroll till you select "None" for symbols and "0" for the number of decimal places. Variations in currency formats are described in the Customized Formatting section.

Your worksheet should now resemble Exhibit 3.7.

EXHIBIT 3.7
LOAN PAYMENTS WORKSHEET

	A	B	C	D
1	Rate	10%	5%	6%
2	Years	10	20	8
3	Principal	$ 100,000.00	$ 30,000.00	$ 20,000.00
4	Annual Payment	($16,274.54)	($2,407.28)	($3,220.72)

COMMAS

The icon of a comma automatically inserts commas into the appropriate places. The columns will automatically widen to accommodate the numerical formatting.

CUSTOMIZED FORMATTING

If you need a format other than what the icons provide, you can customize the formatting of a cell through the menu bar by using the following instructions.

1.   Highlight the cells to be formatted.
2.   Click on Format in the menu bar and select "Cells."
3.   Choose the category and options you desire.

Exhibit 3.8 displays some of the variations in numeric formatting.

EXHIBIT 3.8
EXAMPLES OF AVAILABLE NUMERIC FORMATS

Format Type   **Display**

Number   1234
                         1,234.00 (any number of decimal places may be chosen)
                         -1,234.56 (negative number can also be in parenthesis or in red)

Date   3/14
                         3/14/98
                         March - 98
                         March 14, 1998
                         3/14/98 1:30 PM
                         Some options have the time displayed along with the date.

Time   13:30
                         1:30 PM
                         13:30:55

Percentage   5% or 5.00% (any number of decimal places may be chosen)

Currency $1,234
                         $1,234.00 (any number of decimal places may be chosen)
                         $(1,234.56) negative number

Special   Numbers can be formatted as zip codes, phone numbers, or
                         social security numbers.

Charts 4

The spreadsheet program allows you to create charts or graphs as a way to visually represent numeric data. Excel refers to both charts and graphs as simply "charts." Before creating a chart, the data which is to be used in the chart must be typed into a worksheet. Next, you highlight the data and click on the Chart Wizard icon (a bar chart with blue, yellow, and red columns). The Chart Wizard will guide you through a four step process for creating a chart. A chart is linked to the worksheet data and is automatically updated when the data in the worksheet is changed. The following sections give specific directions on creating different types of charts.

First, set up a new worksheet containing the data in Exhibit 4.1; this data will be used for each of the following charts. Assume that you work for a company which has sales in the United States, Europe, and Asia.

EXHIBIT 4.1
SALES WORKSHEET

	A	B	C	D	E	F
1		SALES BY YEAR AND BY REGION				
2						
3		USA	Europe	Asia	Total Sales	
4	2002	534	231	69		
5	2001	518	146	71		
6	2000	427	75	44		
7	1999	405	239	22		
8	1998	267	119	36		
9	1997	188	84	25		
10						

Use the Autosum icon to total the sales for each year. Review: Highlight the row containing the first year's sales (cells B4 through D4). Click on Autosum and the total will automatically be entered into the next cell (E4). Remember to save time by copying the formula (cell E4) into the remaining cells (cells E5 to E9). Review: Click on the cell which contains the formula (E4). Put the cursor on the small box in the bottom right corner of the cell; the cursor will turn to a "+". Drag the cell over the range of cells you want to fill.

In the latest version of Excel, a green triangle may appear which indicates that a message corresponds to that cell. In this case, Excel is notifying us that the formula did not sum all of the cells in the row (we intentionally did not include the cell containing the year).

COLUMN CHART

A column chart, like a line chart, is a one-dimensional chart. Assume your boss wants to see a comparison of each region's sales over the past six years. You decide to use a column chart. First, highlight the data range which contains the information that will be plotted, in this case that would be the columns containing the years and each region's sales, including their titles (i.e., cells A3 through D9). The headings are being included so that Chart Wizard can use them in the chart legend. Next, click on the Chart Wizard icon. It will present the following four steps:

Step 1.   Select a specific chart type. For this example, select Column chart. Then you will be able to choose from several chart sub-types. Choose the first sub-type box which is labeled "clustered column." Click on "Next."

Step 2.   In this step, Chart Wizard is confirming the data range which you previously highlighted and the fact that your data is in columns. There is a display showing what your chart currently looks like. Click on "Next."
Note: By default, Chart Wizard plots whatever there is fewer of - rows or columns - as the data series. Since our example has fewer columns, the columns containing sales figures were automatically plotted as data series. Chart Wizard uses the first column as the x-axis IF it does not have a heading AND the remaining columns do. Thus, the column containing the years was automatically used for the x-axis instead of being plotted as another data series.

Step 3.   Several chart enhancing options are made available here. Type a title into the title box. Type "Year" into the x-axis box and "Sales" into the y-axis box. These are the only selections necessary for this example. Click on "Next."

Step 4.   Chart Wizard places the chart into your current worksheet unless you select the option of placing it into a new sheet. Click "Finish" and your chart will appear on your worksheet.

When completed, your column chart should resemble Exhibit 4.2. The chart can be repositioned on the worksheet by clicking on it and dragging it to a new position. The chart box can be enlarged by clicking and expanding its borders like any other box.

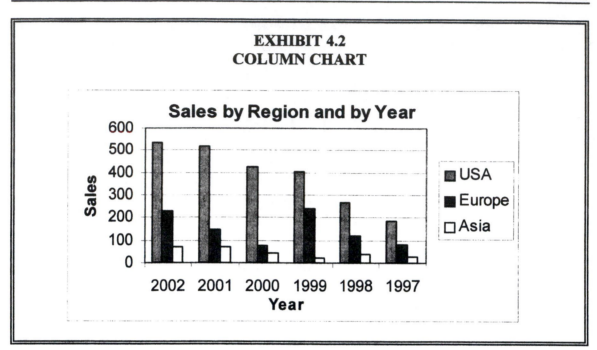

EXHIBIT 4.2
COLUMN CHART

To print a chart, highlight it and select "Print" or "Print-preview." Print-preview allows you to first make setup changes such as size and page orientation (portrait or landscape). To delete a chart from your worksheet, simply click on the chart and press the Delete key.

STACKED-COLUMN CHART

A stacked-column chart is one variation of a column chart. Instead of placing bars next to each other, it stacks shaded bars for multiple ranges of data on top of each other. Try charting the same data range using the stacked-column chart. Click on the Chart Wizard icon and follow the four step process previously described. After selecting the column chart type, we chose the second chart sub-type labeled "stacked column." Your chart should resemble the stacked-column chart in Exhibit 4.3.

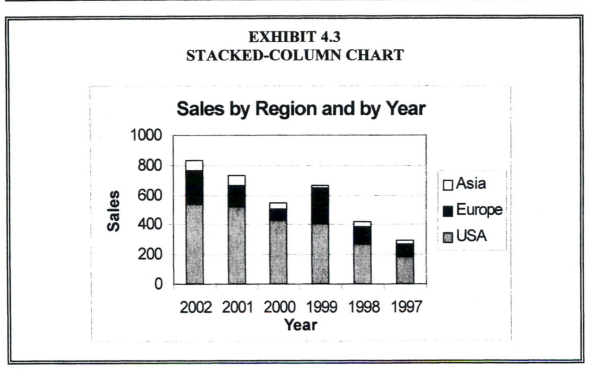

EXHIBIT 4.3
STACKED-COLUMN CHART

LINE CHART

A line chart is used for plotting data on a vertical y-axis and a horizontal x-axis. The y-axis can contain from one to six ranges, producing one to six lines.

Suppose the boss wants to see the total sales trend over the past six years. You decide to use a line chart. The same four step process using Chart Wizard will be used, but this time we will describe some additional options. Highlighting the data range needed for the chart is a bit more difficult since the Total Sales column is not lined up next to the years in the worksheet. We could move the columns around on the worksheet, but instead we will select the x-axis values through the Chart Wizard process. First, highlight the Total Sales column (cells E3 through E9). Next, click on Chart Wizard.

Step 1.   Select the Line chart option. For the sub-type, we chose the first box in the second row which is labeled "Line with markers displayed." Click on "Next."

Step 2.   Chart Wizard is confirming our data range. There is a tab titled "Series," click on that tab. You'll see that Total Sales is listed as a data series. (If we had not highlighted the heading, it simply would be labeled Series 1. You could rename the data series at this point by typing a name into the "Name" box.)

At the bottom of the menu box, you'll see that the x-axis has not been designated. Click on the empty box beside "category (X) axis labels" and then, while still in chart wizard, highlight the years on your worksheet (cells A4 to A9). The range address will automatically be inserted into the box. Click on "Next."

Step 3.   Type in a chart title and axis labels. Click on the tab at the top marked "Data Labels." You are given options as to how to label the plotted line(s). Click on the option "show value." The sales values will appear on your chart. Chart Wizard will automatically show a chart legend unless you turn the option off in this step. Click on "Next."

Step 4.   Chart Wizard places the chart into your current worksheet unless you select the option of placing it into a new sheet. If you choose a new sheet, you can access the different sheets by clicking on the tabs at the bottom of the worksheet.

Exhibit 4.4 contains the line chart just created.

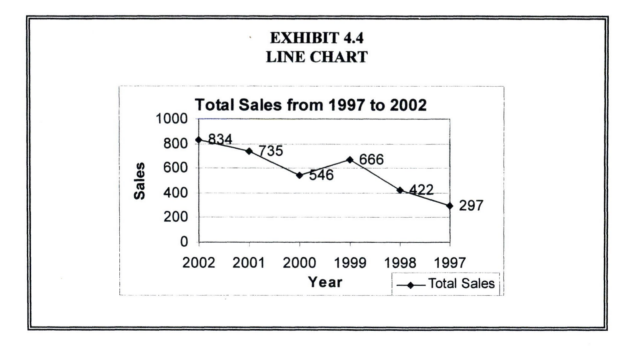

EXHIBIT 4.4
LINE CHART

After you have created the chart, changes can be made to the style of its various parts by right-clicking on the specific part and choosing to re-format. For example, the following changes were made to the chart in Exhibit 4.4.

- The background area of the chart was changed to white by right-clicking on the chart area and accessing the Format Plot Area menu box. Several colors and border styles are made available.

- The style of the plotted lines can be modified by right clicking on the line and accessing the Format Data Series. The style and color of the line can then be changed.

- Excel automatically positions the category labels (Years) between the tick marks on the x-axis and thus plots the values between the tick marks. You can change this and create a direct alignment by right-clicking on the category axis (x-axis) and bringing up the Format Axis menu box, as shown in Exhibit 4.5. Next, click on the "Scale" tab and un-check the box next to "Value (Y) axis crosses between categories."

EXHIBIT 4.5
FORMAT AXIS MENU BOX - SCALE TAB

Format Axis   ? X

| Patterns | Scale | Font | Number | Alignment |

Category (X) axis scale

Value (Y) axis crosses
  at category number: [1]

Number of categories
  between tick-mark labels: [2]

Number of categories
  between tick marks: [1]

☐ Value (Y) axis crosses between categories
☐ Categories in reverse order
☐ Value (Y) axis crosses at maximum category

[OK]   [Cancel]

PIE CHART

A pie chart can be used to graph only a single range of data (i.e., one column or one row of values). For this example, we'll chart the sales for the year 2002 only. First, highlight the **row** containing the 2002 sales data, and include the row containing the regional titles (cells B3 through D4). Click on Chart Wizard and follow the four step process. Under pie chart, we selected the second sub-type choice labeled "pie with a 3-D visual effect." In step 3, we chose to use percentages and names as data labels for the pie slices. We deleted the legend box.

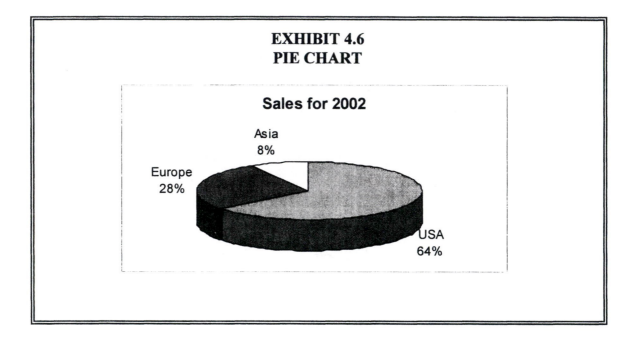

EXHIBIT 4.6
PIE CHART

Sales for 2002

Asia 8%

Europe 28%

USA 64%

Worksheet Manipulation   **5**

RANGE NAMES

Sometimes keeping track of the cell addresses to be included in a range can be quite tedious. Excel provides a command to name ranges and thus refer to the cell addresses by that name. Using range names is useful in sorting, formatting, copying, and printing.

We'll use the sales worksheet from Chapter 4 to practice creating a range name. The worksheet is shown in Exhibit 5.1. Suppose you frequently print the USA's sales figures and, thus, it would save time to use a range name instead of always highlighting the cells.

EXHIBIT 5.1
SALES WORKSHEET

	A	B	C	D	E
1	SALES BY YEAR AND BY REGION				
2					
3		USA	Europe	Asia	Total Sales
4	2002	534	231	69	834
5	2001	518	146	71	735
6	2000	427	75	44	546
7	1999	405	239	22	666
8	1998	267	119	36	422
9	1997	188	84	25	297

Create a range name for the USA column by following these steps:

1.   Highlight the cells that you want to name as a range (B3 through B9). (Note: If you include the title when you initially highlight the range,

Excel will automatically insert the title as the range name.)

2.   Click on "Insert" in the menu bar and select the Name option. Then select "Define."

3.   The name you selected will appear, or you can type in a new name. Click on "OK."

Click on a blank cell to remove the highlighting. Now click on the arrow within the cell designation panel (the box directly above column A). As shown in Exhibit 5.2, this will reveal any ranges which have been named. Click on the "USA" range name which you just created; this causes the USA column to be highlighted. Once a range name has been created, you may use this name anywhere that requires a cell address.

EXHIBIT 5.2
CELL DESIGNATION PANEL

	USA	Europe	Asia	Total Sales
SALES BY YEAR AND BY REGION				
	USA	Europe	Asia	Total Sales
2002	534	231	69	834
2001	518	146	71	735
2000	427	75	44	546
1999	405	239	22	666
1998	267	119	36	422
1997	188	84	25	297

FREEZE PANES

When working on a large worksheet, sometimes the entire worksheet does not fit on the screen. The Freeze Panes command allows you to freeze rows or columns. The cells on one side of the freeze line remain stationary, while the cells on the other side of the line can be scrolled. For example, a row of headings can be frozen while you scroll and view the remainder of the worksheet. Exhibit 5.3 illustrates freezing row 3 of our example worksheet; note that row 3 has remained at the top of the display, while the remaining worksheet has been scrolled to row 9.

EXHIBIT 5.3
FREEZE PANES

	A	B	C	D	E	F
1		SALES BY YEAR AND REGION				
2						
3		USA	Europe	Asia	Total Sales	
9	1997	188	84	25	297	
10						

The Freeze Panes command allows you to compare any rows or columns of data which are not already adjacent on the worksheet.

To use the Freeze Panes option, perform the following steps:

1. Click on the cell where you want the freeze to be. (For our example, A4.)
    a. For a **horizontal** freeze, the rows **above** the cell will be frozen. Click on the first cell of the row.
    b. For a **vertical** freeze, the columns to the **left** of the cell will be frozen. Click on the first cell of the column.
2. Click on "Window" in the menu bar and select the Freeze Panes option.

If you do not click on the first cell in the row or column, then you will achieve horizontal and vertical splits simultaneously. To remove the freeze, click on "Window" and select the Unfreeze Panes option.

SPLIT SCREEN

Under "Window" in the menu bar, there is an option called "Split." This is very similar to freezing panes. The only difference is that the part of the worksheet chosen to remain constant can also be duplicated on the screen by scrolling past it. (The freeze panes option does not duplicate the constant part of the worksheet.) To create a split screen, follow the directions for freeze panes except chose "Split" instead of "Freeze Panes."

IMPORTING DATA

Using the Clipboard feature, you are able to copy or "import" data from other spreadsheets or programs into your Microsoft Excel worksheet.

1. Open the file which contains the data you want imported into your Excel worksheet. Highlight the data that you want copied and copy it to the Clipboard by clicking on the copy icon (2 sheets of paper).
2. Select the area on the Excel worksheet to where the information should be imported and click on the Paste icon (clipboard).

Database Tools **6**

Excel has several features which improve the ease of manipulating data in a worksheet. This chapter specifically covers data form, data sort, Autofill, and Autofilter.

Excel provides a database function which allows you to assimilate and manipulate related information. A **database** is comprised of **records** which are comprised of **fields**. Fields are items such as an account title, an account number, or amount. Fields are made up of alphabetic characters (e.g. account title) or numbers (e.g. amount). Fields that are related are grouped together in records. For example, an accounts receivable record typically includes a field for account number, customer name, and balance. All the accounts receivable records comprise the database (customarily referred to as the accounts receivable master file).

Prepare a new worksheet with the data contained in Exhibit 6.1 using the following Excel feature called "data form."

DATA FORM

The purpose of data form is to reduce errors resulting from entering data into the wrong cell. When using data form, you provide Excel with the titles you want on the worksheet and it inserts these titles into a simplified form. You can then add information record by record. To duplicate the example worksheet using data form, perform the following steps:

1. Type the titles (i.e., account, name, balance, past due) into your worksheet. Refer to Exhibit 6.1 for the exact placement.
2. Highlight the titles. Click on "Data" in the menu bar and choose the "Form" option. You will be asked if the top row of your selection is the header row. Click on "OK."
3. The form will automatically appear with your titles as the field names on the form. You can now begin entering data from your records. IMPORTANT: Use the TAB key when moving from one field to the next. After inserting all the data for one person (a record), hit the Enter key.

Notes: Column B will need to be widened to accommodate the names. At this time, leave the "Account" field blank. When all the records are entered, click on Close. When you are finished, your worksheet should resemble Exhibit 6.1.

EXHIBIT 6.1
EXAMPLE ACCOUNTS WORKSHEET

	A	B	C	D	E
1	Account	Name	Balance	Past Due	
2		Miller, Rob	600	80	
3		Smith, John	220	20	
4		Jackson, Al	50	10	
5		King, James	200	60	
6		Brown, Amy	100	90	
7		Jones, Sara	145	40	
8					

DATA SORT

SORTING A SINGLE COLUMN OR ROW

Excel will sort numbers or words in an ascending or descending manner. The "sort ascending" icon displays the letter A on top of the letter Z; it will sort a list going from A to Z. The "sort descending" icon displays the letter Z on top of the letter A. A column can be sorted by simply clicking on any cell within the column and then clicking on the sort icon. Excel will prioritize alphabetic sorting over numeric sorting.

SORTING MULTIPLE COLUMNS OR ROWS

Suppose the boss wants to view the accounts receivable past due from shortest time past due to longest time past due. In this case, multiple columns need to be sorted in order to keep each person's record intact. Sorting is a bit more entailed since we want to sort by a specific column of numbers (past due amounts). Using your example worksheet, perform the following steps:

1. Highlight each record (i.e. cells B2 through D7).
2. Click on Data in the menu bar and choose "sort." Select the column by which you want the list sorted (past due). Excel gives you the option to sort ascending or descending; choose ascending.

Exhibit 6.2 shows the records by past due values in ascending order.

EXHIBIT 6.2
EXAMPLE ACCOUNTS WORKSHEET

	A	B	C	D
1	Account	Name	Balance	Past Due
2		Jackson, Al	50	10
3		Smith, John	220	20
4		Jones, Sara	145	40
5		King, James	200	60
6		Miller, Rob	600	80
7		Brown, Amy	100	90
8				

Now we will sort the worksheet in a different way using the data sort icon. Suppose the boss wants the list of names alphabetized in the worksheet. Again, to keep each person's record intact, multiple columns need to be sorted. Since Excel will prioritize alphabetic sorting over numeric sorting, it will automatically sort by the Names column (we do not need to specify a column). To alphabetize the records, performing the following steps:

1.   Highlight the appropriate cells (B2 through D7).
2.   Click on the "sort ascending" icon (picture of the letter A on top of the letter Z, with a down arrow along side of it).

Exhibit 6.3 shows the records alphabetized in ascending order.

EXHIBIT 6.3
RESULTS OF DATA SORT

	A	B	C	D
1	Account	Name	Balance	Past Due
2		Brown, Amy	100	90
3		Jackson, Al	50	10
4		Jones, Sara	145	40
5		King, James	200	60
6		Miller, Rob	600	80
7		Smith, John	220	20
8				

AUTOFILL

This command enables the user to fill a specified range with a sequence of numbers or text. Suppose you want to create a consecutive numbering system for customer account numbers, beginning with account number 1001 up to account number 1006. Perform the following steps:

1. Type the first two values of the series (i.e., 1001, 1002) into the first two cells of your list. (Refer to Exhibit 6.4.)
2. Highlight the two cells. Put the cursor on the small box in the bottom right corner of the cell (the fill handle); the cursor will turn to a "+".
3. Drag the cell over the range of cells you want to fill. Release the mouse and AutoFill will automatically fill in the series of cells.

The result of this procedure is displayed in Exhibit 6.4.

EXHIBIT 6.4
RESULTS OF AUTOFILL

	A	B	C	D
1	Account	Name	Balance	Past Due
2	1001	Brown, Amy	100	90
3	1002	Jackson, Al	50	10
4	1003	Jones, Sara	145	40
5	1004	King, James	200	60
6	1005	Miller, Rob	600	80
7	1006	Smith, John	220	20
8				

AUTOFILTER

This command permits the user to select and view records in a database which meet a specific criteria set forth by the user. You determine your criteria by selecting what data from which fields you want to keep. For example, you may choose to view only those records for people who are 40 days or more past due. AutoFilter will allow you to do this by performing the following steps:

1. Highlight all of the records including the titles.

2. Click on "Data" in the menu bar. Choose the Filter option and then the AutoFilter.

3. Small boxes with down arrows will appear in each cell containing a field title. These drop boxes will list options when the arrow is clicked.

4. In order to view only those records that are 40 days or more past due, click on the down arrow in the Past Due cell. Several options will appear, choose the Custom option. (If you selected one of the numbers displayed, than only those records containing that number would be shown.)

5. In the Custom AutoFilter menu box, click on the arrow within the first box in order to view your options. Select the "is greater than or equal to" option. Then, click on the next box to the right and type in "40." Click the OK button.

Your worksheet should now display only those records that are 40 days or more past due, as shown in Exhibit 6.5. To delete the AutoFilter, once again click on Data, then Filter, and uncheck the AutoFilter option by clicking on it.

EXHIBIT 6.5
RESULTS OF AUTOFILTER

Acct	Name	Balance	Past Du
1001	Brown	100	90
1003	Jones	145	40
1004	King	200	60
1005	Miller	600	80

Macro Commands 7

Macros are shortcuts which allow you to reduce a series of different commands or keystrokes into a couple of simple clicks of the mouse. Microsoft Excel allows you to "record" the instruction of several commands and then replay or "run" the macro to activate the commands exactly as you performed them. Macros are efficient in performing time-consuming functions which are done frequently.

CREATING A MACRO

To illustrate the macro feature, we will use the example worksheet which was created in Chapter 6 and is shown below in Exhibit 7.1.

EXHIBIT 7.1
EXAMPLE ACCOUNTS WORKSHEET

	A	B	C	D
1	Account	Name	Balance	Past Due
2	1001	Brown, Amy	100	90
3	1002	Jackson, Al	50	10
4	1003	Jones, Sara	145	40
5	1004	King, James	200	60
6	1005	Miller, Rob	600	80
7	1006	Smith, John	220	20
8				

Suppose the boss wants the accounts sorted according to each person's balance; going from largest to smallest. Since the account balances change often, let's create a macro that runs the sort procedure. The following steps describe how to create a simple macro, in this case, for sorting a worksheet.

1.   Turn on the macro recorder by clicking on "Tools" in the menu bar

and choosing the Macro option and then "Record New Macro."

2. Enter a name for your macro in the Name box. You may replace the name Excel automatically inserted (Macro1) with a name of your choosing, such as "Sort." Click on "OK."

3. A small box will appear on your worksheet labeled "Stop." The macro program will record every action you perform from now until the time you press the blue button in the box.

4. Perform the task you want done. In this case, perform the sort feature: Highlight all the records, but not the titles (i.e. highlight cells A2 to D7). If the box is in the way, it can be moved by clicking on the title and moving the cursor. Click on "Data" in the menu bar and choose "Sort." In the Sort box, select the Balance column in descending order. Click on "OK."

5. Click on the blue button in the Stop box.

Your worksheet should now resemble Exhibit 7.2.

EXHIBIT 7.2
SORTED BY BALANCE USING A MACRO

	A	B	C	D
1	Account	Name	Balance	Past Due
2	1005	Miller, Rob	600	80
3	1006	Smith, John	220	20
4	1004	King, James	200	60
5	1003	Jones, Sara	145	40
6	1001	Brown, Amy	100	90
7	1002	Jackson, Al	50	10

RUNNING A MACRO

Let's make use of the macro we just created. Suppose the account balances have changed in the past week. John Smith reduced his balance down to $120 and James King reduced his balance down to $80. Insert these new figures into your worksheet. Now we'll resort the accounts using the macro. To run the macro, perform the following steps:

1. Select "Tools" in the menu bar and choose the Macro option and then "Macros."

2.   Choose the macro program you want and click on "Run."

This sorting task was relatively simple, but it illustrates the potential that macros have in saving time on tasks that must be constantly repeated.

Guidelines for **8** *Worksheet Design*

The following general guidelines should be considered when designing a worksheet; each will be discussed within this chapter.

1. Outline worksheet requirements (i.e., input and output).
2. Create a file identification area.
3. Establish data input areas separate from output areas.
4. Enter data in rows or columns, but not both.
5. Use manual recalculation when working with large files.
6. Create backup files.
7. Test the worksheet.

REQUIREMENTS OUTLINE

The first guideline in creating a worksheet is to outline the worksheet requirements. What input is necessary to solve the problem at hand? What output is required? These requirements should be determined before beginning work. For example, assume you are required to create a worksheet that projects income statements for the next two years based on a constant growth rate in sales revenue. In this case, the required input is the current sales amount, annual sales growth rate, cost of goods sold as a percentage of sales, and the fixed amount of operating expenses.

The output requirement would be projected income statements for the next two years.

FILE ID

A file identification area should be prepared at the top of the worksheet. Prepare a new worksheet with the following file identification information: the file name, the worksheet designer's name, the input required, the output generated, and the dates the file was created, modified, and last used. See Exhibit 8.1 for an illustration.

EXHIBIT 8.1
FILE IDENTIFICATION AREA

	A	B	C	D	E
1	IDENTIFICATION AREA:				
2					
3	Filename: Forecast				
4	Designer:				
5	Input Required:				
6		a. Current sales amount			
7		b. Annual sales growth rate			
8		c. Cost of goods sold as a % of sales			
9		d. Operating Expenses			
10	Output: Projected Income Statements				
11	File Created:				
12	File Modified:				
13	Last Used:				
14					

DATA INPUT

The data items necessary for using the worksheet are typed into one column of the input area. For this example, cost of goods sold is assumed to be a constant percentage of sales and operating expenses are assumed to be a fixed amount each year. The input area for our example worksheet is illustrated in Exhibit 8.2. Enter these input items along with their respective values into your worksheet. Be sure to put the values into column E. (We will be inserting formulas later with the cell address of E.)

Formulas within the output area are based upon values in the input area. This enables the user to modify any value in the input area and instantly see how the change affects the output.

EXHIBIT 8.2
FILE ID AND INPUT AREA

	A	B	C	D	E
1	IDENTIFICATION AREA:				
2					
3	Filename:Forecast				
4	Designer:				
5	Input Required:				
6	a. Current sales amount				
7	b. Annual sales growth rate				
8	c. Cost of goods sold as a % of sales				
9	d. Operating Expenses				
10	Output: Projected Income Statements				
11	File Created:				
12	File Modified:				
13	Last Used:				
14					
15					
16	INPUT AREA:				
17					
18	Current sales ($):				1,000
19	Growth rate as a % of sales:				12%
20	Cost of goods sold as a % of sales:				60%
21	Operating expenses ($):				100
22					

DATA OUTPUT

The output area of the worksheet contains the desired results. The output for our example is projected income statements for the next two years. Exhibit 8.3 displays the output area items and formulas. Type these into your worksheet. For purposes of this example, the income statement is limited to only five line items. Exhibit 8.4 shows the computation results. Note: For uniformity, we formatted the income statements amounts to include two decimal places. This was easily accomplished by highlighting the appropriate cells and then clicking on the "increase decimal" icon (an arrow next to ".0"). Decimal places can also be specified by clicking on "Format" in the menu bar, as discussed in Chapter 3.

EXHIBIT 8.3
FILE ID, INPUT AND OUTPUT AREAS

	A	B	C	D	E
1	IDENTIFICATION AREA:				
2					
3	Filename:Forecast				
4	Designer:				
5	Input Required:				
6	a. Current sales amount				
7	b. Annual sales growth rate				
8	c. Cost of goods sold as a % of sales				
9	d. Operating Expenses				
10	Output: Projected Income Statements				
11	File Created:				
12	File Modified:				
13	Last Used:				
14					
15					
16	INPUT AREA:				
17					
18	Current sales ($):				1,000
19	Growth rate as a % of sales:				12%
20	Cost of goods sold as a % of sales:				60%
21	Operating expenses ($):				100
22					
23					
24	OUTPUT AREA:				
25					
26	Projected Income Statement for the Next Two Years				
27					
28				20x1	20x2
29					
30	Sales			=E18+E18*E19	=D30+D30*E19
31	Cost of goods sold			=D30*E20	=E30*E20
32					
33	Gross Profit			=D30-D31	=E30-E31
34	Operating Expenses			=E21	=E21
35					
36	Projected Net Income			=D33-D34	=E33-E34

EXHIBIT 8.4
OUTPUT AREA RESULTS

24	OUTPUT AREA:		
25			
26	Projected Income Statement for the Next Two Years		
27			
28		20x1	20x2
29			
30	Sales	1120.00	1254.40
31	Cost of goods sold	672.00	752.64
32			
33	Gross Profit	448.00	501.76
34	Operating Expenses	100.00	100.00
35			
36	Projected Net Income	348.00	401.76

Once the output area is formatted by typing in the required items and formulas, the computations are totally formula driven, based upon values in the input area. As previously noted, this enables the user to modify any value in the input area and instantly see how the change affects the output. For example, change the growth rate percentage in the input area from 12% to 15%; you will instantly see the recalculations resulting in a net income of $360 for the first year and $429 for the second year.

INPUT ALIGNMENT

For maximum efficiency, the input cells should be aligned vertically (in a column) or horizontally (in a row), but not both. Fewer mistakes should occur if the user doesn't have to steer the cursor through a maze of input cells.

MANUAL RECALCULATION

If more than one value in the input area is to be changed on a large worksheet, it is helpful to turn off Excel's automatic recalculation. This is due to the fact that the software instantly recalculates mathematical expressions once a value has been modified. Data cannot be entered while the recalculations are taking place. The time involved is inconsequential for small worksheets but can become a burden for large worksheets. A simple procedure is used to change from automatic recalculation to manual recalculation:

1.   Click on "Tools" in the menu bar and choose "Options."
2.   Select the Calculation tab.
3.   In the Calculation area, click on "Manual."

In the Manual mode, when a value in the input area is changed, the output values will not change in response. If you wish for Excel to recalculate an amount, without reinstating the automatic recalculation option, you can press the F9 key. Excel will recalculate for the values currently in the worksheet. When using manual recalculation, a good idea is to type a note on the worksheet that you must press "F9" to recalculate.

BACKUP FILES

Backup copies should be continually updated and stored in more than one place. When creating a worksheet, the user should periodically (every 15 to 30 minutes) save the file in case of a power outage or other event that may cause erasure of the file and the loss of hours of work.

TESTING

Any new worksheet should be manually tested. If formulas are involved, the user must test the worksheet result against an example that is already proven correct.

Step-by-Step Excel Example   *9*

This chapter provides step-by-step instructions for creating a simple worksheet and graph using Microsoft Excel spreadsheet software.

CREATING AN EXCEL WORKSHEET

Open a new worksheet and enter the information shown in Exhibit 9.1. Brief reviews of some of the Excel features are given if you should need them. Note that the sales amount of 1000 dollars must be placed in cell C6.

EXHIBIT 9.1
EXAMPLE WORKSHEET

	A	B	C	D	E	F
1	IDENTIFICATION AREA:					
2	Filename: Example					
3	Designer:					
4						
5	INPUT AREA:					
6	Sales in $ =		1000			
7						
8	OUTPUT AREA:					
9			JACOB & SISTERS BRICK COMPANY			
10			INCOME STATEMENT			
11		For the Year Ended December 31, 20x1				
12						
13	Sales					
14	Cost of sales					
15	Gross profit					
16	Operating expense					
17	Net Income					
18						

EDITING A CELL

A cell can be put into edit mode by double clicking on the cell. Excel will then allow you to move around within the cell and change the contents. After you are finished typing, press "Enter" to insert the contents into the worksheet. If you want to delete the entire contents of a cell, click on the cell and press the delete key.

CENTERING

After the company name and income statement headings are typed in, they are centered by highlighting each row individually from A to E (e.g. A9 to E9) and then clicking on the centering icon (the letter "a" between arrows pointing left and right).

INSERTING FORMULAS

Formulas are entered just as they would be processed algebraically, using cell addresses to represent values in the equation. When an equal sign is the very first thing entered, Excel knows this cell contains a mathematical expression. (If there is a space before the equal sign, Excel will read it as text.)

Assume that the company expects sales of $1,000 for the year ended 12/31/x1. The cost of sales is expected to be 60 percent of sales and operating expenses average 10 percent of sales. Using this information, we can create formulas for each of the items on our worksheet. Type the formulas from Exhibit 9.2 into your worksheet; press "Enter" after each entry.

EXHIBIT 9.2
FORMULAS FOR EXAMPLE WORKSHEET

	A	B	C	D	E
8	OUTPUT AREA:				
9		JACOB & SISTERS BRICK COMPANY			
10		INCOME STATEMENT			
11		For the Year Ended December 31, 20x1			
12					
13	Sales		=C6		
14	Cost of sales		=C13*.60		
15	Gross profit		=C13-C14		
16	Operating expense		=C13*.10		
17	Net Income		=C15-C16		

Your worksheet should now contain the correct values for each item, as shown in Exhibit 9.3

EXHIBIT 9.3
EXAMPLE WORKSHEET - OUTPUT

8	OUTPUT AREA:		
9	JACOB & SISTERS BRICK COMPANY		
10	INCOME STATEMENT		
11	For the Year Ended December 31, 20x1		
12			
13	Sales	1000	
14	Cost of sales	600	
15	Gross profit	400	
16	Operating expense	100	
17	Net Income	300	
18			

MANIPULATING DATA

The worksheet just created can be used for any amount of sales by simply changing the value for sales in the input area. The computations in the output area are totally formula driven, based on amounts in the input area. This enables the user to modify any value in the input area and instantly see how the change affects the output. For example, change the value of sales from $1000 to $2000 in the input area; click on cell C6 and type in 2000. You'll note that each item in the output area was automatically recalculated and the new net income is $600.

NUMERIC FORMATTING

If you wish to include dollar signs and commas, click on the cells containing currency. Once the cells are selected, click on the icon of a dollar sign ($). Alternatively, you can click on "Format" in the menu bar and then select "Cells - Number - Currency."

COLUMN EXPANSION

When the spreadsheet program is first loaded, the column width will be eight characters. If your cell data exceeds the cell width, the data will simply run into the adjacent empty cell; this is what occurred in our example worksheet. However, if the adjacent cell is not empty, the overflow data will be truncated at the cell border. To avoid this, column width can be changed using the following steps. Note: It is best to be out of the edit mode when changing cell width; click on a blank cell to exit the edit mode.

1.   Position the cursor at the top of the screen on the mid-point between the lettered column headings (i.e., between A and B). The cursor should change into a "+."
2.   Click-and-drag using the left mouse key; hold it while "dragging" the column to a different width.

PRINTING

For printing your worksheet, it is helpful to first highlight the section you want printed and then click on "File" in the menu bar. Select "Print." Under the print options, choose "Selection." Another very useful step is to select "File - Print Preview" to see how your output will look. By skipping these steps, and depending on where the cursor is, you could print several pages unnecessarily.

CREATING AN EXCEL PIE CHART

Before creating a chart, the data which is to be used in the chart must be typed into a worksheet. Next, you highlight the data and click on the Chart Wizard icon (picture of blue, yellow, and red columns on a bar chart). The Chart Wizard will guide you through a four step process for creating a chart. A chart is linked to the worksheet data it's created from and is automatically updated when the data in the worksheet is changed

We'll prepare a pie chart of the division of sales revenue using Chart Wizard. A pie chart can be used to graph only a single range of data (i.e., one column or one row of values). Use the values corresponding with sales of $2000. Skip down a couple of lines on your worksheet and type in the data as shown in Exhibit 9.4.

EXHIBIT 9.4
SCHEDULE OF DATA FOR PIE CHART

	A	B	C
20	Cost of sales		1200
21	Operating expense		200
22	Net Income		600

Highlight the data range which contains the information that will be charted (C20 to C22). Next, click on the Chart Wizard icon. It will present the following four steps:

Step 1.   Select a specific chart type. For this example, select Pie chart. Then you will be able to choose from several chart sub-types. Choose the first sub-type box which is labeled "Pie." Click on "Next."

Step 2.   In this step, Chart Wizard is confirming the data range which you previously highlighted and the fact that your data is in columns. There is a display showing what your chart currently looks like. There is a tab titled "Series," click on that tab. Here, we can insert labels for our pie slices. Click on the empty box next to "Category Labels" at the bottom. Then, while still in chart wizard, highlight the labels on your worksheet (cells A20 to A22 containing the words "cost of sales, operating expense, net income"). The range address will automatically be inserted into the box. Click on "Next."

Step 3.   Several chart enhancing options are made available here. Type a title into the title box. Under the Data Labels tab, we choose "show percent." Click on "Next."

Step 4.   Chart Wizard places the chart into your current worksheet unless you select the option of placing it into a new sheet. Click "Finish" and your chart will appear on your worksheet.

   Your pie chart should resemble Exhibit 9.5. The chart can be repositioned on the worksheet by clicking on it and dragging it to a new position. The chart box can be enlarged by clicking and expanding its borders like any other box.

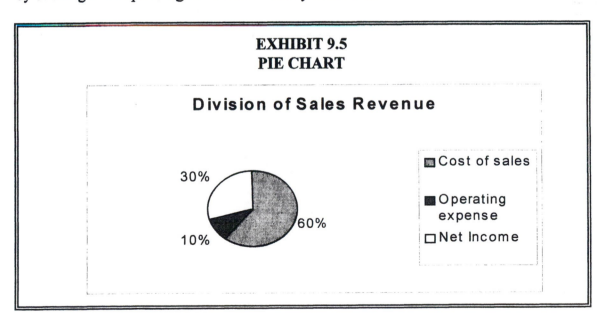

EXHIBIT 9.5
PIE CHART

Division of Sales Revenue

30%

10%

60%

■ Cost of sales

■ Operating expense

□ Net Income

Spreadsheet Assignments

LIST
of Spreadsheet Assignments

The list below provides a brief description of each assignment and related accounting topic area. Solutions to selected assignments are shown at the end of the book. In addition, a number of example worksheet files are available on the book's website (IOLBV.com/murphy/EXCEL4ACCT1).

* Indicates that the solution to the assignment is at the end of this book.

ACCOUNTING TOPIC	No.	DESCRIPTION
Accounting and the	1*	Income Statement
Business Environment	2	Cost of Goods Sold
	3	Financial Statements
	4	Income Statement
	5	Statement of Owner's Equity
Recording Business Transactions	6	Double-Entry Accounting
	7	Double-Entry Accounting
	8	T-Accounts and Trial Balance
	9	Trial Balance and Income Statement
Measuring Business Income:	10	Preparation of adjusted trial balance
The Adjusting Process	11	Financial Statements and Related Questions
Completing the Accounting Cycle	12	Post Closing Trial Balance
	13	Trial Balance and Worksheet
Merchandising Operations and	14	Sales by Product Type
the Accounting Cycle	15	Balance Sheet
	16	Financial Ratios
Accounting Information Systems	17	Cash Disbursements
Internal Control and Managing Cash	18*	Cash Budget
	19	Cash Budget
	20	Bank Reconciliation
	21	Cash Budget

ACCOUNTING TOPIC	**No.**	**DESCRIPTION**
Accounts and Notes Receivable	22*	Bad Debt Expense
	23	Bad Debt Expense
	24	Aging Sales Invoices
	25	Aging Sales Invoices
	26	Aging Sales Invoices
	27	Statement of Cash Flows
Accounting for Merchandise Inventory	28	Cost of Merchandise
	29	Cost of Merchandise
	30*	Tracking Inventory Quantity
	31	Product Cost Schedule
	32	Income Statement
	33	Perpetual Inventory Record
	34	Income Statement, Balance Sheet, & Statement of Cash Flows
Plant Assets, Intangibles Assets, and Related Expenses	35	Straight Line Depreciation
	36	Straight Line Depreciation
	37	Sum-of-the-Years-Digits Deprec.
	38	Units-of-Production Depreciation
	39	Joint Cost Allocation
	40*	Joint Cost Allocation
	41	Allocation of Costs in Lump-Sum Purchase
Current Liabilities and Payroll Acctg.	42	Partial Balance Sheet
Accounting for Partnerships	43	Summary of Liquidation Transactions
Corporate Organization, Paid-In Capital, and the Balance Sheet	44*	Weighted Average Number of Shares of Stock
	45	Financial Ratios
	46	Balance Sheet, Financial Ratios, and Related Questions
Retained Earnings, Treasury Stock, and Income Statement	47	Multiple-Step Income Statement

ACCOUNTING TOPIC	No.	DESCRIPTION
Long-Term Liabilities	48	Lease Payment
	49	Bond Amortization Schedule
Accounting for Investments and International Operations	50*	Interest Earned
	51	Future Value of a Single Deposit
	52	Foreign Currency Translation Using Current Rate Method
	53*	Foreign Currency Translation Using Current Rate Method
	54	Foreign Currency Translation Using Current Rate Method
	55	Foreign Currency Translation Using Current Rate Method
	56	Foreign Currency Translation Using Temporal Rate Method
	57	Foreign Currency Translation Using Temporal Rate Method
	58	Economic Impact of Import Quota
	59	Economic Impact of Import Quota
	60	Economic Impact of a Tariff
	61	Economic Impact of a Tariff
	62	Economic Impact of a Tariff
Statement of Cash Flows	63	Statement of Cash Flows -- Investing Activities
	64	Statement of Cash Flows
Financial Statement Analysis	65	Financial Ratios
	66	Financial Ratios
	67	Common Size Balance Sheets
	68	Common Size Balance Sheets
	69	Horizontal Analysis of Income Statement

1. INCOME STATEMENT

Create an Income Statement for Chris Ray's Card Shop for year ended 12/31/x1. See Chapter 9 for an example. Assume that sales are expected to be $200,000. The cost of sales is 40% of sales and operating expenses are 15% of sales. The income statement should include the following line items: sales, cost of sales, gross profit, operating expenses, and net income. Note: The solution to this problem is at the end of the book.

2. COST OF GOODS SOLD

Create the following cost of goods sold statement.

DORIS' DIAMOND CO.
COST OF GOODS SOLD
For Year Ended 12/31/x2

Beginning Inventory	$100,000
Purchases	50,000
Goods Available	$150,000
Ending Inventory	75,000
Cost of Goods Sold	$ 75,000

3. FINANCIAL STATEMENTS

Examine Exhibits A and B. Exhibit A summarizes the eleven transactions of Gary Lyon, CPA, for the month of April 20x1. Suppose Lyon has completed the first seven transactions only and needs a bank loan on April 21, 20x1. The vice president of the bank requires financial statements to support all loan requests.

    Prepare the income statement, statement of owner's equity, and balance sheet that Gary Lyon would present to the banker after completing the first seven transactions on April 21, 20x1. Exhibit B shows the financial statements on April 30.

EXHIBIT A
Analysis of Transactions of Gary Lyon, CPA

	Assets						
	Cash	+	Accounts Receivable	+	Supplies	+	Land
(1)	+ 50,000						
Bal.	50,000						
(2)	- 40,000						+40,000
Bal.	10,000						40,000
(3)					+500		
Bal.	10,000				500		40,000
(4)	+ 5,500						
Bal.	15,500				500		40,000
(5)			+3,000				
Bal.	15,500		3,000		500		40,000
(6)	- 1,100						
	- 1,200						
	- 400						
Bal.	12,800		3,000		500		40,000
(7)	- 400						
Bal.	12,400		3,000		500		40,000
(8)	Not a transaction of the business						
(9)	+ 1,000		- 1,000				
Bal.	13,400		2,000		500		40,000
(10)	+22,000						- 22,000
Bal.	35,400		2,000		500		18,000
(11)	- 2,100						
Bal.	33,300		2,000		500		18,000	=	53,800

EXHIBIT A (cont.)

	Liabilities	+	Owner's Equity	Type of Owner's Equity Transaction
	Accounts Payable	+	Gary Lyon, Capital	
(1)			+ 50,000	*Owner investment*
Bal.			50,000	
(2)			————	
Bal.			50,000	
(3)	+ 500		————	
Bal	500		50,000	
(4)			+ 5,500	*Service revenue*
Bal.	500		55,500	
(5)	————		+ 3,000	*Service revenue*
Bal.	500		58,500	
(6)			- 1,100	*Rent expense*
			- 1,200	*Salary expense*
			- 400	*Utilities expense*
Bal.	500		55,800	
(7)	- 400			
Bal.	100		55,800	
(8)				
(9)	————		————	
Bal.	100		55,800	
(10)	————		————	
Bal.	100		55,800	
(11)	————		- 2,100	*Owner withdrawal*
	100		53,700	= 53,800

EXHIBIT B
Financial Statements of Gary Lyon, CPA

Gary Lyon, CPA
Income Statement
Month Ended April 30, 20x1

Revenue:

Service revenue $8,500

Expense:

Salary expense	$1,200	
Rent expense	1,100	
Utilities	400	
Total expenses		2,700
Net income		$5,800

Gary Lyon
Statement of Owner's Equity
Month Ended April 30, 20x1

Gary Lyon, capital, April 1, 20x1	$ 0
Add: Investments by owner	50,000
Net income for the month	5,800
. . . .	55,800
Less: Withdrawals by owner	(2,100)
Gary Lyon, capital, April 30, 20x1	$53,700

Gary Lyon, CPA
Balance Sheet
April 30, 20x1

Assets		**Liabilities**	
Cash	$33,300	Accounts payable	$ 100
Accounts receivable	2,000		
Office supplies	500	**Owner's Equity**	
Land	18,000	Gary Lyon, capital	53,700
		Total liabilities and	
Total assets	$53,800	owner's equity	$53,800

Gary Lyon, CPA
Statement of Cash Flows*
Month Ended April 30, 20x1

Cash flows from **operating** activities:

Receipts:
  Collections from customers ($5,500 + $1,000).. $ 6,500

Payments:
  To suppliers ($1,100 + $400 + $400)................ $(1,900)
  To employees.......................................   (1,200)   (3,100)
    Net cash inflow from operating activities........   3,400

Cash flows from **investing** activities:
  Acquisition of land................................ $(40,000)
  Sale of land.......................................   22,000
    Net cash outflow from financing..................   (18,000)

Cash flows from financing activities:
  Investment by owner................................ $ 50,000
  Withdrawal by owner................................   (2,100)
    Net cash inflow from financing activities.......   47,900
Net increase in cash................................. $33,300
Cash balance, April 1, 20x1..........................   0
Cash balance, April 30, 20x1......................... $33,300

*Refer to your textbook for more information regarding this statement.

4.   INCOME STATEMENT

On-Point Delivery Service has just completed operations for the year ended December 31, 20x3. This is the third year of operations for the company. As the proprietor of the business, you want to know how well the business performed during the year. You also wonder where the business stands financially at the end of the year. To address these questions, you have assembled the following data:

Salary expense	$32,000	Insurance expense	$ 4,000
Accounts payable	7,000	Service revenue	91,000
Owner, capital		Accounts receivable	17,000
December 31, 20x2	13,000	Supplies expense	1,000
Supplies	2,000	Cash	5,000
Withdrawals by owner	36,000	Fuel expense	6,000
Rent expense	8,000		

Prepare the income statement of On-Point Delivery Service for the year ended December 31, 20x3. Follow the format shown in Exhibit B of Assignment 3. The income statement will measure the business's performance for the year.

5. STATEMENT OF OWNERS' EQUITY

Use the data in the assignment above to prepare the statement of owner's equity of On-Point Delivery Service for the year ended December 31, 20x3. Follow the format shown in Exhibit B of Assignment 3. Compute net income from data provided in the prior assignment.

6. DOUBLE-ENTRY ACCOUNTING

Design a worksheet that enables the user to record transactions in general ledger accounts. Additionally, the worksheet should be designed so that the ending balances in the general ledger accounts are used to automatically prepare a trial balance and an income statement, which will be prepared in the next assignment. Use the same approach as shown in the example file, GLEDGER, which is available on the book's website (IOLBV.com/murphy/excel4acct1). Starting with a zero balance in all general ledger accounts, enter the following transactions. Print the general ledger.

Jan. 1:	Mary Smith opens a consulting firm with an $8,000 deposit into the firm's checking account.
Jan. 1:	Prepaid three months of rent for $1,500.
Jan. 2:	Borrowed $4,000 with a note payable to purchase a computer with a two-year useful life and a salvage value of $400.
Jan. 3:	Purchased office supplies on credit for $800.
Jan. 10:	Provided consulting services on account for $3,200.
Jan. 12:	Provided consulting services on account for $1,200.
Jan. 15:	Received partial payment of $1,600 for services rendered on account on January 10.
Jan. 20:	Provided consulting services on account for $2,000.

Jan. 25:	Paid telephone bill of $375.
Jan. 26:	Paid electric bill of $225.
Jan. 31:	Make adjusting entry to record expiration of one month of prepaid rent.
Jan. 31:	Make adjusting entry to record use of office supplies. One-half of supplies have been used.
Jan. 31:	Record depreciation on office equipment for one month. Use straight-line depreciation.
Jan. 31:	The owner, Mary Smith, withdraws $4,000 for personal use.

7.   DOUBLE-ENTRY ACCOUNTING

Using information from the prior assignment, print the trial balance and income statement.

8.   T-ACCOUNTS AND TRIAL BALANCE

Refer to the following transactions of Wellness Health Club.

Wellness Health Club Transactions

Wellness Health Club engaged in the following transactions during March 20x3, its first month of operations:

Mar. 1	Lou Stryker invested $45,000 of cash to start the business.
2	Purchased office supplies of $200 on account.
4	Paid $40,000 cash for a building to use as a future office.
6	Performed service for customers and received cash, $2,000.
9	Paid $100 on accounts payable.
17	Performed service for customers on account, $1,600.
23	Received $1,200 cash from a customer on account.
31	Paid the following expenses: salary, $1,200; rent, $500.

Record the preceding transactions in the journal of Wellness Health Club. Key transactions by date and include an explanation for each entry. Use the following accounts: Cash; Accounts Receivable; Office Supplies; Building; Accounts Payable; Lou Stryker, Capital; Service Revenue; Salary Expense; Rent Expense. (Hint: For help, refer to the example file, GLEDGER, on the website.)

1.   After journalizing the above transactions, post the entries to the ledger, using T-account format. Key transactions by date. Date the ending balance of each account Mar. 31.

2.   Prepare the trial balance of Wellness Health Club at March 31, 20x3.

9. TRIAL BALANCE & INCOME STATEMENT

The following trial balance for Cincinnati Landscaping Service does not balance:

Cincinnati Landscaping Service
Trial Balance
June 30, 20x2

Cash..	$ 2,000	
Accounts receivable..............	10,000	
Supplies................................	900	
Equipment............................	3,600	
Land......................................	46,000	
Accounts payable...................		$ 4,000
Note payable.........................		22,000
Margo Schotte, capital...........		31,600
Margo Schotte, withdrawals..	2,000	
Service revenue......................		6,500
Salary expense.......................	2,100	
Rent expense.........................	1,000	
Advertising expense...............	500	
Utilities expense....................	400	
Total......................................	$68,500	$64,100

The following errors were detected:
a. The cash balance is understated by $700.
b. The cost of the land was $43,000, not $46,000.
c. A $200 purchase of supplies on account was neither journalized nor posted.
d. A $2,800 credit to Service Revenue was not posted.
e. Rent expense of $200 was erroneously posted as a credit rather than a debit.
f. The balance of Advertising Expense is $600, but on the trial balance it was $500.
g. A $300 debit to Accounts Receivable was posted as $30.
h. The balance of Utilities Expense is overstated by $70.
i. A $900 debit to the Withdrawals account was posted as a debit to Margo Schotte, Capital.

1.   Prepare the correct trial balance at June 30. Journal entries are not required.
2.   Prepare the company's income statement for the month ended June 30, 20x2, in order to determine Cincinnati Landscaping Service's net income or net loss for the month. Refer to Exhibit B of Assignment 3 if needed.

10. PREPARATION OF ADJUSTED TRIAL BALANCE

The adjusted trial balance of Total Express Service is incomplete. Enter the adjustment amounts directly in the adjustment columns. Service Revenue is the only account affected by more than one adjustment.

	Total Express Service Preparation of Adjusted Trial Balance May 31, 20X2						
	Trial Balance		Adjustments		Adjusted Trial Balance	
Account Title	Debit	Credit	Debit	Credit	Debit	Credit
Cash	3,000				3,000	
Accounts receivable	6,500				7,100	
Supplies	1,040				800	
Office furniture	32,300				32,300	
Accumulated depreciation		14,040				14,400
Salary payable						900
Unearned revenue		900				690
Capital		26,360				26,360
Owner's withdrawals	6,000				6,000	
Service revenue		11,630				12,440
Salary expense	2,690				3,590	
Rent expense	1,400				1,400	
Depreciation expense					360	
Supplies expense					240	
	52,930	52,930			54,790	54,790

11.   FINANCIAL STATEMENTS AND RELATED QUESTIONS

The adjusted trial balance of Tradewind Travel Designers at December 31, 20x6 follows:

Tradewind Travel Designers
Adjusted Trial Balance
December 31, 20x6

Cash	$ 1,320	
Accounts receivable	8,920	
Supplies	2,300	
Prepaid rent	1,600	
Office equipment	20,180	
Accumulated depreciation-office equipment		$ 4,350
Office furniture	37,710	
Accumulated depreciation-office furniture		4,870
Accounts payable		3,640
Property tax payable		1,100
Interest payable		830
Unearned service revenue		620
Note payable		13,500
Gary Gillen, capital		26,090
Gary Gillen, withdrawals	29,000	
Service revenue		124,910
Depreciation expense-office equipment	6,680	
Depreciation expense-office furniture	2,370	
Salary expense	39,900	
Rent expense	17,400	
Interest expense	3,100	
Utilities expense	2,670	
Insurance expense	3,810	
Supplies expense	2,950	
Total	$179,910	$179,910

Prepare Tradewind's 20x6 income statement and statement of owner's equity and year-end balance sheet. List expenses in decreasing order on the income statement and show total liabilities on the balance sheet.

1.   Which financial statement reports Tradewind Travel's results of operations? Were operations successful during 20x6? Cite specifics from the financial statements to support your evaluation.

2.   Which statement reports the company's financial position? Does Tradewind's financial position look strong or weak? Give the reason for your evaluation.

12.   POST-CLOSING TRIAL BALANCE

After closing its accounts at December 31, 20x6, Sprint Corporation had the following account balances, with amounts given in millions:

Property and equipment	$10,464	Long-term liabilities	$5,119
Cash	1,150	Other assets	2,136
Service revenue	-0-	Accounts receivable	2,464
Owners' equity	8,520	Total expenses	-0-
Other current assets	739	Accounts payable	1,027
Short-term notes payable	200	Other current liabilities .	2,087

Prepare Sprint's post-closing trial balance at December 31, 20x6. List accounts in proper order, like the trial balance shown below.

Gary Lyon, CPA
Postclosing Trial Balance
April 30, 20x1

Cash	$24,800	
Accounts receivable	2,500	
Supplies	400	
Prepaid rent	2,000	
Furniture	16,500	
Accumulated depreciation		$ 275
Accounts payable		13,100
Salary payable		950
Unearned service revenue		300
Gary Lyon, capital		31,575
Total	$46,200	$46,200

13. TRIAL BALANCE AND WORKSHEET

The trial balance of Goldsmith Testing Service follows:

Goldsmith Testing Service
Trial Balance
September 30, 20x6

Cash	$ 3,560	
Accounts receivable	3,440	
Prepaid rent	1,200	
Supplies	3,390	
Equipment	32,600	
Accumulated depreciation		$ 2,840
Accounts payable		3,600
Salary payable		
L. Goldsmith, capital		36,030
L. Goldsmith, withdrawals	3,000	
Service revenue		7,300
Depreciation expense		
Salary expense	1,800	
Rent expense		
Utilities expense	780	
Supplies expense		
Total	$49,770	$49,770

Additional information at September 30, 20x6:
     Accrued service revenue, $210.
     Depreciation, $40.
     Accrued salary expense, $500.
     Prepaid rent expired, $600.
     Supplies used, $1,650.

Complete Goldsmith's worksheet (on the following page) for September 20x6.

Account Title	Trial Balance		Adjust- ments		Adjusted Trial Bal.		Income Statement		Balance Sheet	
Goldsmith Testing Service **Work Sheet** **Month Ended September 30, 20X6**										
	Dr.	Cr.	Dr.	Cr.	Dr.	Cr.	Dr.	Cr.	Dr.	Cr.
Cash										
Accounts receivable										
Prepaid rent										
Supplies										
Equipment										
Accumulated depreciation										
Accounts payable										
Salary payable										
L. Goldsmith, capital										
L. Goldsmith, withdrawals										
Service revenue										
Depreciation expense										
Salary expense										
Rent expense										
Utilities expense										
Supplies expense										
Totals										
Net income										
Totals (IS, BS)										

14.   SALES BY PRODUCT TYPE

Using the data below in the input area, prepare a new report sorted by current-month sales.

SALES SUMMARY REPORT BY PRODUCT TYPE
February

Product Type	Current Month Sales	Prior Month Sales	% Chg.	Year to Date Sales	Last Yr. YTD Sales	% Chg.
A	16	25	-36%	80	100	-20%
B	52	45	16%	260	234	11%
C	44	32	38%	220	154	43%
D	72	67	7%	360	333	8%
E	35	37	-5%	175	180	-3%

15.   BALANCE SHEET

Use the data shown below to prepare Bell Computer's balance sheet at January 31, 20x5. Use the report format with all headings and list accounts in proper order.

Bell Computer Corporation

Bell Computer Corporation reported these figures in its January 31, 20x5 financial statements (in millions):

Cash	$ 43	Other assets (long-term)	$ 7
Total operating expenses	589	Other current liabilities	304
Accounts payable	447	Property and equipment	208
Owners' equity	652	Net sales revenue	3,475
Long-term liabilities	191	Other current assets	596
Inventory	293	Accounts receivable	538
Cost of goods sold	2,737	Accumulated depreciation	91

16.   FINANCIAL RATIOS

Refer to the Bell Computer situation shown above. Compute Bell's gross margin percentage and rate of inventory turnover for 20x5. One year earlier, at January 31, 20x4, Bell's inventory balance was $220 million.

17.   CASH DISBURSEMENTS

During February, PanAm Imports had the following transactions:

Feb.   3   Paid $392 on account to Marquis Corp. net of an $8 discount for an earlier
             purchase of inventory.
        6   Purchased inventory for cash, $1,267.
        11   Paid $375 for supplies.
        15   Purchased inventory on credit from Monroe Corporation, $774.
        16   Paid $4,062 on account to LaGrange Associates; there was no discount.
        21   Purchased furniture for cash, $960.
        26   Paid $3,910 on account to Graff Software for an earlier purchase of
             inventory. The discount was $90.
        27   Made a semiannual interest payment of $800 on a long-term note payable.
             The entire payment was for interest.

1.   Prepare a cash disbursement journal similar to the one illustrated below. As shown,
      the check number (Ck. No.) and posting reference (Post. Ref.) columns are not
      included.
2.   Record the transactions in the journal. Which transaction should not be recorded in
      the cash disbursements journal? In what journal does it belong?
3.   Total the amount columns of the journal. Determine that the total debits equal the
      total credits.

Solution Started:

Cash Disbursements Journal					
		Debits		Credits	
Date		Account Debited	Other Accounts	Accounts Payable	Inventory	Cash
Feb.	3	Marquis Corp.		400	8	392

18.   CASH BUDGET

Create a worksheet of the following cash budget:

	MARCH	APRIL
Cash balance, beginning	$10,000	$29,500
Cash collections from customers	25,000	15,000
Sale of an asset	12,000	0
Total Available	$47,000	$44,500
Cash disbursements:		
Purchases	$12,000	$ 8,000
Operating expenses	5,500	2,225
Total Disbursements	$17,500	$10,225
Cash balance, ending	$29,500	$34,275

Note: The solution to this problem is at the end of the book.

19.   CASH BUDGET

Refer to the assignment above, but assume that the beginning cash balance on March 1 is now $15,000 and purchases are $10,000 (not $8,000) in April. Recompute the cash budget.

20.   BANK RECONCILIATION

D.J. Hunter's checkbook lists the following:

Date	Check No.	Item	Check	Deposit	Balance
9/1					$ 525
4	622	La Petite French Bakery	$ 19		506
9		Dividends Received		$ 116	622
13	623	General Tire Co.	43		579
14	624	Exxon Oil Co.	58		521
18	625	Cash	50		471
26	626	Fellowship Bible Church	25		446
28	627	Bent Tree Apartments	275		171
30		Paycheck		1,800	1,971

Hunter's September bank statement shows the following:

Balance			$525
Add: Deposits			116
Deduct checks:	No.	Amount	
	622	$19	
	623	43	
	624	68*	
	625	50	(180)

Other charges:

Printed checks	$ 8	
Service charge	12	(20)
Balance		$441

*This is the correct amount for check number 624.
Prepare Hunter's bank reconciliation at September 30.

21. CASH BUDGET

Suppose Sprint Incorporated, the long-distance telephone company, is preparing its cash budget for 20x4. The company ended 20x3 with $126 million, and top management forsees the need for a cash balance of at least $125 million to pay all bills as they come due in 20x4.

Collections from customers are expected to total $11,813 million during 20x4, and payments for the cost of services and products should reach $6,166 million. Operating expense payments are budgeted at $2,744 million.

During 20x4, Sprint expects to invest $1,826 million in new equipment, $275 million in the company's cellular division, and to sell older assets for $116 million. Debt payments scheduled for 20x4 will total $597 million. The company forecasts net income of $890 million for 20x4 and plans to pay $338 million to its owners.

Prepare Sprint's cash budget for 20x4. Will the budgeted level of cash receipts leave Sprint with the desired ending cash balance of $125 million, or will the company need additional financing?

22.   BAD DEBT EXPENSE

Use the following information to calculate bad debt expense for 20x1:

Age of Accounts	A/R Balance	Percent Uncollectible
Under 30 days	$45,000	1%
31-60 days	25,000	3%
61-120 days	15,000	10%
Over 120 days	10,000	30%
Total	$95,000	

Prepare a worksheet demonstrating your computations. Note: The solution to this problem is at the end of the book.

23.   BAD DEBT EXPENSE

Now, assume that bad debt expense is 1% of credit sales. Using the following information, design a worksheet to calculate bad debt expense for 20x1:

Sales during 20x1:		
	Cash Sales	$100,000
	Credit Sales	200,000
	Total Sales	$300,000

24.   AGING SALES INVOICES

Design a worksheet which will enable the user to enter information from uncollected sales invoices. The information should include invoice number, date, amount, firm, and term. The worksheet should be able to calculate the number of days past due for each invoice (account receivable). It should also produce an aging schedule based on days past due. You need to include a line for the current date on the worksheet. You can use the command "=today( )" to make this always show the actual date, but we will enter the date so that it can be changed manually. In future assignments, we will experiment with different dates to see what happens with the aging analysis. For this assignment, use 11/15/03 as the date. Enter the date as "=date(03,11,15)."

A simple formula should be used to find the number of days outstanding for each receivable. To do this, simply subtract the sales invoice date from the current date shown on the worksheet. This will indicate the number of days that have elapsed since the invoice date;

then subtract this number from the number of days in the term (e.g. 30 or 60, as in n/30 or n/60). The result is the number of days past due. Last, sort the invoices by days past due.

The input area should include the following uncollected invoices:

	A	B	C	D	E	F	G	H	I
9	Input Area:								
10	Date:	11/15/03							
11									
12	Invoice #	Date	Amount	Firm		Terms			
13	225	5/25/03	$950	blue	1	10	N	60	
14	301	6/17/03	235	red	2	10	N	60	
15	302	7/2/03	340	red	2	10	N	60	
16	303	7/3/03	560	blue	1	10	N	60	
17	307	8/18/03	270	pink			N	60	
18	309	9/15/03	880	pink			N	30	
19	312	9/22/03	1690	blue	1	10	N	60	
20	317	10/2/03	120	pink			N	30	
21	318	10/3/03	490	pink			N	30	
22	319	10/7/03	460	blue	1	10	N	60	

Use the following layout for the output area:

	A	B	C	D	E	F	G	H	I	J
25	Output Area:									
26										
27									Days	Days
28	Invoice #	Date	Amount	Firm		Terms			O/S	Past Due
29	225	5/25/03	$950	blue	1	10	N	60	174	114
30										

25.   AGING SALES INVOICES

Same assignment as the prior assignment, but in the output area, add a row at the bottom showing average days for terms, days outstanding, and days past due.

26.   AGING SALES INVOICES

Using the worksheet created in Assignment 24, change the date to November 1, 2003. Print the revised aging schedule.

27.   STATEMENT OF CASH FLOWS

The Home Depot, Inc. is the world's largest home improvement retailer. One of the company's great strengths is its cash flow from operations. The Home Depot has been able to grow rapidly without having to borrow heavily. This problem will sharpen your understanding of cash flows reporting.

At January 31, 20x7, end of the company's fiscal year, The Home Depot reported the following items in its financial statements (amounts in millions):

Net sales	$19,536	Notes receivable	$39,518
Cash	146	Loaned out money on	
Cash receipts of interest		notes receivable	1,342
(same as interest revenue)	26	Merchandise inventories	2,708
Buildings	2,470	Accounts receivable, net	388
Cost of goods sold	14,101	Collections on notes receivable	16,539
Collections from customers	19,473	All other expenses	4,523

1. Show how The Home Depot could have reported the relevant items from this list on its statement of cash flows for the year ended January 31, 20x7. Include a heading for the statement.
2. Compute The Home Depot's net income for the year. Was all the net income received in cash? How can you tell?

28.   COST OF MERCHANDISE

Design a worksheet which will compute the cost of merchandise purchased. The worksheet should show the cost with and without the discount. The discount should be shown as the difference between these two amounts. Assume that you have purchased merchandise with a gross price of $5,000. This merchandise is subject to a trade discount of 30%. The trade discount is subtracted from the gross price to determine your actual purchase price. The credit terms offered to your company are 2/10 net 30. What is the amount due assuming that you do not take advantage of the discount period? What do you owe if you do take advantage of the discount?

29.   COST OF MERCHANDISE

Same as above assignment, but use $10,000 worth of merchandise rather than $5,000.

30.   TRACKING INVENTORY QUANTITY

Design a worksheet which will enable you to enter inventory data. The information should include an item number, description, quantity on hand, and quantity desired. The worksheet should then calculate the amount by which the quantity on hand is above or below the desired quantity by use of a formula. Use the following information to complete the worksheet:

Item No	Description	Quantity on hand	Quantity desired
100	HAMMER	8	30
200	SCREWDRIVER	26	20
300	SAW	57	45
400	WRENCH	34	20
500	PLIERS	5	15

Note: The solution to this problem is at the end of the book.

31.   PRODUCT COST SCHEDULE

Prepare a cost schedule for Austin Company for Product X and Product Y using the following layout:

(Input Area)		Product X	Product Y
	Total Units		
	DM Cost/Unit		
	DL Cost/Unit		
	OH allocation rate		
	Total OH (X & Y)		

(Output Area)

                        Company Name
                     Product Cost Schedule
                            Date

		Product X	Product Y
	Direct Materials		
	Direct Labor		
	Manufacturing Overhead		
	Total Cost		

The costs of the direct material for the two products are $2.00 per unit for X and $3.00 per unit for Y. The direct labor costs are $.25 per unit produced for either product. The total manufacturing overhead for the year is $300,000. This should be allocated to the different products based on the ratio of each product's production to total production. Austin Company produced 100,000 units of product X and 50,000 units of product Y.

32. INCOME STATEMENT

Supply the missing income statement amounts, a-g, for each of the following companies:

Company	Net Sales	Beginning Inventory	Net Purchases	Ending Inventory	Cost of Goods Sold	Gross Margin
A	$92,800	$12,500	$62,700	$19,400	(a)	$37,000
B	(b)	27,450	93,000	(c)	$94,100	51,200
C	94,700	(d)	54,900	22,600	59,400	(e)
D	98,600	10,700	(f)	8,200	(g)	47,100

Prepare the income statement for Company D, which uses the periodic inventory system. Company D's operating expenses for the year were $32,100.

33. PERPETUAL INVENTORY RECORD

Piazza Music World carries a large inventory of guitars, keyboards, and other musical instruments. Because each item is expensive, Piazza uses a perpetual inventory system. Company records indicate the following for a particular line of Casio keyboards:

Date	Item	Quantity	Unit Cost
May 1	Balance	5	$90
6	Sale	3	
8	Purchase	11	95
17	Sale	4	
30	Sale	1	

Determine the amounts that Piazza should report for ending inventory and cost of goods sold by the FIFO method. Prepare the perpetual inventory record for Casio keyboards, using the model that follows.

Perpetual Inventory Record – FIFO Cost

	Hunting Galleries								
Item: Early American Chairs									
	Received			Sold			Balance		
Date	Qty.	Unit Cost	Total	Qty.	Unit Cost	Total	Qty.	Unit Cost	Total
Nov.									
1							10	$300	$3,000
5				6	$300	$ 1,800	4	300	1,200
7	25	$310	$7,750				4	300	1,200
							25	310	7,750
12				4	300	1,200			
				9	310	2,790	16	310	4,960
26	25	320	8,000				16	310	4,960
							25	320	8,000
30				16	310	4,960			
				5	320	1,600	20	320	6,400
Totals:	50		$15,750	40		$12,350	20		$6,400

34. INCOME STATEMENT, BALANCE SHEET, AND STATEMENT OF CASH FLOWS

Campbell Soup Company uses a perpetual inventory system and the LIFO method to determine the cost of its inventory. During a recent year, Campbell Soup reported the following items in its financial statements, year ended July 31, 20x5 (listed in alphabetical order, and with amounts given in millions of dollars).

Collections from customers	$7,255	Payments for inventory ..	$4,150
Cost of goods sold	4,264	Revenues, total	7,288
Other expenses	2,326	Total assets	6,315
Owners' equity	2,468	Total liabilities	3,847

1. Prepare as much of Campbell Soup Company's statement of cash flows for the year ended July 31, 20x5, as you can. Include a complete heading.
2. Prepare Campbell Soup Company's income statement for the year ended July 31, 20x5, complete with a heading.
3. Prepare Campbell Soup Company's balance sheet at July 31, 20x5, complete with a heading.

35. STRAIGHT-LINE DEPRECIATION

Design a worksheet that will enable you to compute the annual depreciation expense of a fixed asset using the straight-line method. Assume ABC company bought a machine on July 1 of this year for $20,000. ABC expects the machine to have a useful life of ten years and a $2,000 salvage value at the end of that time. Calculate depreciation expense for this machine in the current year assuming a December 31 year-end.

36. STRAIGHT-LINE DEPRECIATION

Same as above but the salvage value is changed from $2,000 to $4,000; and the machine was purchased on October 1 rather than July 1.

37. SUM-OF-THE-YEARS-DIGITS DEPRECIATION

Design a worksheet which will allow you to calculate the sum-of-the-years-digits depreciation on equipment for the current year. Assume that you bought a machine on January 1 of Year 1 for $250,000. It is expected to have a $24,000 salvage value. Its useful life is estimated to be 10 years. You are completing the financial statements for the year ended December 31, Year 4. What is the SYD depreciation that should be included as an expense for Year 4? The following formula can be used to compute SYD Depreciation: =SYD(COST,SALVAGE,LIFE,PERIOD).

38. UNITS-OF-PRODUCTION DEPRECIATION

Create a worksheet which will calculate deprecation on a machine based on the units-of-production method of depreciation. Assume that you bought a machine on January 1 of Year 1 for $150,000. It has a $2,000 salvage value and a useful life of 100,000 units. Calculate the depreciation expense, accumulated depreciation, and net machine (cost less accumulated depreciation) that would be shown on the balance sheet for the first three years of use based on the following information:

	UNITS PRODUCED
1ST year	15,000
2ND year	20,000
3RD year	18,000

39.   JOINT COST ALLOCATION

You are performing an audit on a small company and must ensure that the total joint costs are allocated correctly among the three products of the company. Use the following information to compute the cost allocated to each product. NOTE: Total costs to be allocated are $450,000.

Product	Sales Value at Split-Off
A	$500,000
B	300,000
C	200,000

Prepare a worksheet demonstrating your computations.

40.   JOINT COST ALLOCATION

Referring to the prior exercise, calculate the joint costs to be allocated to the three products assuming that total costs are $600,000 and the sales values at split-Off are as follows:

Product	Sales Value at Split-off
A	$800,000
B	500,000
C	700,000

Note: The solution to this problem is at the end of the book.

41.   ALLOCATION OF COSTS IN LUMP-SUM PURCHASE

Advantage Leasing Company bought three used machines in a $40,000 lump-sum purchase. An independent appraiser valued the machines as follows:

Machine No.	Appraised Value
1	14,000
2	18,000
3	16,000

Advantage paid half in cash and signed a note payable for the remainder. Record the purchase in the journal, identifying each machine's individual cost in a separate Machine account. Round decimals to three places.

42.   PARTIAL BALANCE SHEET

Assume that Wilson Sporting Goods completed these selected transactions during December 20x6:

a.   Champs, a chain of sporting goods stores, ordered $15,000 of tennis and golf equipment. With its order, Champs sent a check for $15,000 in advance. Wilson will ship the goods on January 3, 20x7.

b.   The December payroll of $195,000 is subject to employee withheld income tax of 9%, FICA tax of 8% (employee and employer), state unemployment tax of 5.4%, and federal unemployment tax of 0.8 percent. On December 31, Wilson pays employees but accrues all tax amounts.

c.   Sales of $1,000,000 are subject to estimated warranty cost of 1.4 percent.

d.   On December 2, Wilson signed a $100,000 note payable that requires annual payments of $20,000 plus 9% interest on the unpaid balance each December 2nd.

Classify each liability as current or long-term, and prepare a partial balance sheet showing liabilities above, as of December 31, 20x6.

43.   SUMMARY OF LIQUIDATION TRANSACTIONS

Prior to liquidation, the accounting records of Pratt, Qualls, and Ramirez included the following balances and profit-and-loss sharing percentages:

| | | | | | Capital | |
	Cash +	Noncash Assets	= Liabilities	+ Pratt (40%)	+ Qualls (30%)	Ramirez + (30%)
Balances before sale of assets	$8,000	$57,000	$19,000	$20,000	$15,000	$11,000

The partnership sold the noncash assets for $73,000, paid the liabilities, and disbursed the remaining cash to the partners. Complete the summary of transactions in the liquidation of the partnership. Use the same approach as in the illustration that follows.

Partnership Liquidation –
Sale of Assets at a Gain

	Cash	+	Noncash Assets	=	Liabilities	+	Aviron (60%)	+	Bloch (20%)	+	Crane (20%)
Balance before sale of											
Assets	$ 10,000		$90,000		$30,000		$40,000		$20,000		$10,000
Sale of assets and											
sharing of gain	150,000		(90,000)				36,000		12,000		12,000
Balances	160,000		-0-		30,000		76,000		32,000		22,000
Payment of liabilities ..	(30,000)				(30,000)						
Balances	130,000		-0-		-0-		76,000		32,000		22,000
Disbursement of cash											
to partners	(130,000)						(76,000)		(32,000)		(22,000)
Balances	$ -0-		$ -0-		$ -0-		$ -0-		$ -0-		$ -0-

44. WEIGHTED AVERAGE NUMBER OF SHARES OF STOCK

Design a worksheet which will enable you to compute the weighted average number of shares of common stock outstanding during the year. In January, there are 500 shares of common stock outstanding. In April, the company sold 700 additional shares. In August, the company purchased 200 of its shares. In September, it issued 800 shares. In November it bought back 300, and in December it sold 500. Assume that all transactions took place on the first day of the month in which they occurred. If today is December 31, what was the weighted average number of shares outstanding during the year? Note: The solution to this problem is at the end of the book.

45. FINANCIAL RATIOS

DuBois Furniture, Inc., reported these figures for 20x7 and 20x6:

	20x7	20x6
Income statement:		
Interest expense	$ 17,400,000	$7,100,000
Net income	12,000,000	18,700,000
Balance sheet:		
Total assets	351,000,000	317,000,000
Preferred stock, $1.30, no-par,		
100,000 shares issued and outstanding	2,500,000	2,500,000
Common stockholders' equity	164,000,000	151,000,000
Total stockholders' equity	166,500,000	153,500,000

Compute rate of return on total assets and rate of return on common stockholders' equity for 20x7. Do these rates of return suggest strength or weakness? Give your reason.

46. BALANCE SHEET, FINANCIAL RATIOS, AND RELATED QUESTIONS

The following accounts and related balances of Borzhov, Inc. are in no particular order:

Accounts receivable, net	...$46,000	Interest expense		$ 6,100
Paid-in capital in excess		Property, plant, and		
Of par-common	19,000	equipment, net		261,000
Accrued liabilities	26,000	Common stock, $1 par,		
Long-term note payable	42,000	500,000 shares authorized,		
Inventory	81,000	236,000 shares issued	...	236,000
Dividends payable	9,000	Prepaid expenses		10,000
Retained earnings	?	Revenue from donation	...	6,000
Accounts payable	31,000	Common stockholders' equity,		
Trademark, net	9,000	June 30 , 20x1		222,000
Preferred stock, $0.10, no-par		Net income		31,000
10,000 shares authorized		Total assets, June 30, 20x1		404,000
and issued	27,000	Cash		13,000

1. Prepare the company's classified balance sheet in the account format at June 30, 20x2. Use the accounting equation to compute Retained Earnings.
2. Compute rate of return on total assets and rate of return on common stockholders' equity for the year ended June 30, 20x2.
3. Do these rates of return suggest strength or weakness? Give your reason.

47. MULTIPLE-STEP INCOME STATEMENT

Graz Corporation's accounting records contain the following for 20x8 operations:

Sales revenue	$380,000
Operating expenses (including income tax)	93,000
Cumulative effect of change in depreciation method (debit).	(7,000)
Cost of good sold	245,000
Loss on discounted operations	50,000
Income tax expense - extraordinary gain	6,000
Income tax saving-change in depreciation method	3,000
Income tax saving-loss on discontinued operations	20,000
Extraordinary gain	15,000

Prepare a multiple-step income statement for 20x8. Omit earnings per share. Was 20x8 a good year, a fair year, or a bad year for Graz Corporation? Explain your answer in terms of the outlook for 20x9.

48.   LEASE PAYMENT

Create a lease payment schedule based on the following data. Show the payment, interest expense, amortization of principal, and carrying value at December 31 for each year: Year 1 to Year 5.

Carrying value Jan. 1, Year 1	$20,000
Beginning of lease term	Jan. 1, 19Y1
Effective Interest	12%
Term of lease	5 years
Payment, beginning 12/31/Y1	$ 5,548

49.   BOND AMORTIZATION SCHEDULE

Atlas Airlines, Inc., issued $600,000 of an 8 3/8% (0.08375), five-year bonds payable when the market interest rate was 9 1/2% (0.095). Atlas pays interest annually at year end. The issue price of the bonds was $574,082.

Create a spreadsheet model to prepare a schedule to amortize the discount on these bonds. Use the effective-interest method of amortization. Round to the nearest dollar, and format your answer as follows.

	A	B	C	D	E	F
11	Output Area:					
12						Bond
13		Interest	Interest	Discount	Discount	Carrying
14	Date	Payment	Expense	Amortization	Balance	Amount
15	1-1-x1				$	$574,082
16	12-31-x1	$	$	$		$
17	12-31-x2					
18	12-31-x3					
19	12-31-x4					
20	12-31-x5					

Use the following formulas:
Interest payment (B16):	=600000*.08375
Interest expense (C16):	=F15*.095

Discount amortization (D16):   =C16-B16
Discount balance (E15):   =600000-F15
Bond carrying amount (F16):   =F15+D16

50.   INTEREST EARNED

Design a worksheet which will enable you to compute the interest earned on a note. The input area should include the following items:

Principal amount of the note
Interest rate
Length of time the note has been held (# of days)

The output area of the worksheet should calculate the interest earned using the items in the input area. Assume that you purchased a note on November 1 of this year with a principal amount of $1,000. Assume further that the amount you paid equaled the face amount of the note and the annual interest rate is 7 percent. How much interest earned should you report at December 31 of this year assuming that you do not sell the note before the end of the year? Note: The solution to this problem is at the end of the book.

51.   FUTURE VALUE OF A SINGLE DEPOSIT

Create a worksheet which will enable you to compute the length of time required for a lump sum investment made today to grow to a desired future value. For this assignment, assume that you have $40,000 to invest today and that the investment will always earn an 8 percent return. How long must you leave the money in the account before your investment is worth $500,000? Use the following formula: =NPER(Interest Rate,-Present Value, Future Value).

Background for Assignments 52 to 57: Foreign Currency Translation

When a multinational corporation based in the U.S. owns more than 50 percent of the voting stock of a foreign company, a parent-subsidiary relationship exists. The parent company is usually required to prepare consolidated financial statements. Before this can be done, the financial statements of the foreign subsidiary must be recast using U.S. generally accepted accounting principles (GAAP). Next, the foreign accounts must be remeasured (translated) from the foreign currency into U.S. dollars. To make the translation, the first step is to identify three currencies:

(A)   Currency of books and records (CBR) -- the CBR is the currency in which the foreign financial statements are denominated;

(B)   Functional currency (FC) -- the FC is the one in which the subsidiary generally buys, sells, borrows, repays, etc.; and

(C)   Reporting currency (RC) -- the RC is the one in which the consolidated financial statements are denominated.

There are basically three approaches to currency translation: (1) temporal rate method, (2) current rate method, and (3) use of both methods. The following three rules are used to determine the method of translation:

Rule 1:   If the FC is hyper-inflationary (i.e., 100% cumulative inflation within three years), then ignore the FC and remeasure the CBR into the RC using the temporal rate method.

Rule 2:   If the CBR is different from the FC, then remeasure the CBR into the FC using the temporal rate method.

Rule 3:   Translate from the FC into the RC using the current rate method.

You must apply the rules in sequence, stopping when the subsidiary's financial statements have been converted into the parent's reporting currency (RC). For example, when the functional currency (FC) is hyper-inflationary, then Rule 1 applies; that is, the financial statements which are denominated in the CBR are translated into the RC using the temporal rate method, and Rules 2 and 3 aren't used. A second example is as follows: If the CBR is British pounds, the FC is Dutch guilders (not hyper-inflationary), and the RC is U.S. dollars; then you skip Rule 1 and apply Rule 2, translating the CBR (pounds) into the FC (guilders) using the temporal rate method. Since the FC (guilders) is not the RC (dollars), you would then apply Rule 3 to translate the FC (guilders) into the RC (dollars) using the current rate method. A third example is as follows: When the CBR is the same as the FC, then you go directly to Rule 3.

Using the current rate method, all assets and liabilities are translated using the current rate (i.e., exchange rate on the balance sheet date). Owners' equity and dividends are translated at historical rates (exchange rate at the time the asset was acquired, liability incurred, or element of paid-in capital was issued or reacquired). Income statement items can be translated using the average exchange rate (the average of the exchange rate at the beginning of the accounting period and the current rate).

Under the temporal rate method, the objective is to measure each subsidiary transaction as though the transaction had been made by the parent. Monetary items (e.g. cash, receivables, inventories carried at market, payables, and long-term debt) are remeasured using the current exchange rate. Other items (e.g. prepaid expenses, inventories carried at cost, fixed assets, and stock) are remeasured using historical exchange rates.

52. FOREIGN CURRENCY TRANSLATION USING THE CURRENT RATE METHOD

First, read the background information for this problem on the preceding pages. Translate the following account balances from Dutch guilders to U.S. dollars using the current rate method.

Adjusted Trial Balance
In Dutch Guilders (DG)
December 31, Year 4

	Debit	Credit
Cash	20,000	
Accounts Receivable	35,000	
Inventory	105,000	
Equipment	60,000	
Accum. Dep.		20,000
Accounts Payable		35,000
Bonds Payable		50,000
Revenues		120,000
General Expenses	108,000	
Depreciation Expense	8,000	
Dividends	4,000	
Common Stock		62,000
Paid-in Capital in Excess of Par		44,000
Retained Earnings		9,000
Total	340,000	340,000

Exchange Rates:

	1 DG = $___
Current Exchange Rate	0.520
Average Exchange Rate	0.490
At July 31, Year 4	0.505
At June 30, Year 1	0.470

Other: All common stock was issued on June 30, Year 1 (i.e., 6/30/Y1).
Dividends were declared and paid on July 31, Year 4.
Translated Retained Earnings at 12/31/Y4 was: $5,500.

53.   FOREIGN CURRENCY TRANSLATION USING THE CURRENT RATE METHOD

Same as previous assignment, except the exchange rates are as follows:

Current Exchange Rate	1.200
Average Exchange Rate	1.250
At July 31, Year 4	1.300
At June 30, Year 1	1.000

Note: The solution to this problem is at the end of the book.

54.   FOREIGN CURRENCY TRANSLATION USING THE CURRENT RATE METHOD

Use the following information to translate from British pounds to U.S. dollars using the current rate method. Background information is on page 83.

Adjusted Trial Balance
In British Pounds
December 31, Year 8

	Debit	Credit
Cash	72,000	
Accounts Receivable	60,000	
Inventory	136,000	
Fixed Assets	130,000	
Accum. Dep.		76,000
Accounts Payable		50,000
Bonds Payable		90,000
Revenues		172,000
General Expenses	158,000	
Depreciation Expense	10,000	
Dividends	4,000	
Common Stock		58,000
Paid-in Capital in Excess of Par		98,000
Retained Earnings		26,000
Total	570,000	570,000

Exchange Rates:

	1 BP = $___
Current Exchange Rate	2.100
Average Exchange Rate	2.000
At July 31, Year 8	2.050
At June 30, Year 1	1.500

Other:

All common stock was issued on June 30, Year 1 (i.e., 6/30/Y1).
Dividends were declared and paid on July 31, Year 8.
Translated Retained Earnings at 12/31/Y8 was $22,600.

55. FOREIGN CURRENCY TRANSLATION USING THE CURRENT RATE METHOD

Same as previous assignment, except use the following exchange rates:

Current Exchange Rate	3.100
Average Exchange Rate	2.900
At July 31, Year 8	2.950
At June 30, Year 1	4.000

56. FOREIGN CURRENCY TRANSLATION USING THE TEMPORAL RATE METHOD

Use the temporal rate method to remeasure from the currency of books and records (i.e., British pounds) to the functional currency (i.e., U.S. dollars). Background information is on page 83.

Adjusted Trial Balance
In British Pounds
December 31, Year 4

	Debit	Credit
Cash	52,000	
Accounts Receivable	60,000	
Inventory		
(10-31-Y3)	40,000	
(7-31-Y4)	160,000	
Fixed Assets		
(6-30-Y1)	13,000	

(12-31-Y1)	65,000	
(7-31-Y2)	52,000	
Accum. Dep.		
(6-30-Y1)		8,000
(12-31-Y1)		40,000
(7-31-Y2)		32,000
Accounts Payable		43,000
Bonds Payable		160,000
Revenues		214,000˙
General Expenses	189,000	
Depreciation Expense		
(6-30-Y1)	1,500	
(12-31-Y1)	7,500	
(7-31-Y2)	6,000	
Dividends (7-31-Y4)	10,000	
Common Stock		
(6-30-Y1)		48,000
(1-31-Y2)		32,000
Paid-in Capital in Excess of Par		
(6-30-Y1)		30,000
(1-31-Y2)		20,000
Retained Earnings		29,000
Total	656,000	656,000

Exchange Rates:

	1 BP = $___
Current Exchange Rate	0.600
Average Exchange Rate	0.610
At July 31, Year 4	0.606
At October 31, Year 3	0.591
At July 31, Year 2	0.585
At January 31, Year 2	0.586
At December 31, Year 1	0.590
At June 30, Year 1	0.580

Other:

Regarding common stock, 60% was issued 6/30/Y1; 40% on 1/31/Y2.
Regarding inventory, 20% was acquired 10/31/Y3; 80% on 7/31/Y4.
Dividends were declared and paid on 7/31/Y4.
Regarding fixed assets, 10% were acquired 6/30/Y1; 50% on 12/31/Y1; and 40% on 7/31/Y2.

Revenues and expenses were accrued evenly throughout the year.
Translated retained earnings at 12/31/Y4 was $16,400

57.   FOREIGN CURRENCY TRANSLATION USING THE TEMPORAL RATE METHOD

Same as previous assignment, except use the following exchange rates:

	1 BP = $___
Current Exchange Rate	2.000
Average Exchange Rate	2.400
At July 31, Year 4	2.300
At October 31, Year 3	2.150
At July 31, Year 2	2.200
At January 31, Year 2	2.180
At December 31, Year 1	2.250
At June 30, Year 1	2.100

Background for Assignments 58 to 62: Comparative Advantage

Productivity provides an economic basis for trade. During the early 1800s, David Ricardo and other economists provided an explanation for trade based on different levels of productivity among nations in different industries. This can be illustrated as follows. First, assume that there is only one factor of production, labor. Next, assume that a worker in the country of Bigred can produce either 8 bales of cotton or 4 crates of apples, and that a worker in the country of Bigblue can produce either 1 bale of cotton or 1 crate of apples. Table A shows production in Bigred and Bigblue.

Table A
Cotton and Apples as Produced by Bigred and Bigblue

	Bigred Worker	Bigblue Worker
Cotton	8 bales	1 bale
Apples	4 crates	1 crate

Opportunity costs of production are shown in Table B.

Table B
Opportunity Costs of Production in Bigred and Bigblue

Bigred:	8 bales of cotton cost 4 crates of apples, so
	1 bale of cotton costs 1/2 crate of apples.
	4 crates of apples cost 8 bales of cotton, so
	1 crate of apples costs 2 bales of cotton.
Bigblue:	1 bale of cotton costs 1 crate of apples.
	1 crate of apples costs 1 bale of cotton.

Table A shows that a worker in Bigred is more productive in both cotton and apples than a worker in Bigblue. The Bigred worker has an "absolute advantage" in productivity in both industries. When industries are compared, the Bigred worker is found to be relatively more productive in the cotton industry (8 to 1) than in the apple industry (4 to 1) in relation to the Bigblue worker. Thus, the Bigred worker has a "comparative advantage" in the cotton industry. Thus, Bigred's absolute advantage in cotton is proportionately greater than its absolute advantage in apples.

A lower skilled and lower productive nation will have a comparative advantage in something because there will be some industry in which it is least disadvantaged. If Bigred is better at producing apples than Bigblue, why won't Bigred produce its own apples? The answer is that Bigred determines it more advantageous to produce what it does best, cotton, and trading this cotton for apples. Table C, which is derived from Table B, shows what prices would have to be in effect for trade to be beneficial.

Table C
Prices at Which Trade Would Occur

Bigred:	If 1 bale of cotton sells for more than 1/2 crate of apples, Bigred gains by selling cotton.
	If 1 crate of apples sells for less than 2 bales of cotton, Bigred gains by buying apples.
Bigblue:	If 1 bale of cotton sells for less than 1 crate of apples, Bigblue gains by buying cotton.
	If 1 crate of apples sells for more than 1 bale of cotton, Bigblue gains by selling apples.
Thus:	If the price of apples on the world markets is between 1 bale of cotton and 2 bales of cotton, and if the price of apples is between 1/2 crate of apples and 1 crate of apples, trade is mutually advantageous.

Table D shows the change in world output if firms in each nation reallocate workers to the industry in which the nation has a comparative advantage. The Bigred cotton industry hires a worker away from the apple industry, and the Bigblue apple industry hires five workers away from the cotton industry. Consequently, the world output of cotton increases by 3 bales, and the world output of apples increases by 1 crate.

Table D **Increase in World Production Based on Transfers of** **One Worker in Bigred and Five Workers in Bigblue**			
	One Bigred Worker	Five Bigblue Workers	World Output
Cotton (bales)	+1	-5	+3
Apples (crates)	-1	+5	+1

Assume that the Bigred firm exports 4 bales of cotton to Bigblue, and that the price of a bale of cotton is 0.7 crates of apples. The trade yields Bigred 2.8 crates of apples. Before international trade, the Bigred firm could have obtained only 2 crates of apples for its 4 bales of cotton. Before international trade, the Bigblue could have obtained only 2.8 bales of cotton for its 2.8 crates of apples, but now gets 4 bales of cotton for its 2.8 crates. The price determines which country receives the greatest benefit. For example, if 1 bale of cotton equals to 0.8 crates of apples, Bigred would have benefitted more from the trade than where the price was 0.7 crates. However, as long at the price falls within the range shown in Table C, both countries gain from specialization and trade. If the costs of production of cotton and apples remained constant, eventually all cotton would be produced in Bigred and all apples in Bigblue. However, increasing costs will probably occur at some point; the cost of producing cotton in Bigred will increase, and the cost of producing apples in Bigblue will increase. At this point, trade is curtailed. Consequently, it is rarely the case that one country produces all of one product.

Effects of an Import Quota

Given the above presentation of comparative advantage, you can understand why the great majority of economists strongly support free trade and oppose the use of tariffs and quotas that impede the free exchange of goods and services. However, there are political motivations that advocate protection of domestic industry. The political motivations for advocating protectionism generally are not supported by sound economic analysis.

58.   ECONOMIC IMPACT OF AN IMPORT QUOTA

First, read the background information for this problem on page 89.
Use the following equation to prepare a domestic demand curve:
    $P(QD) = 100 - 10 * Q$

Use the following equations to prepare a domestic supply and a world supply curve:
    $P(QS\text{-}d) = 0 + 10 * Q$
    $P(QS\text{-}w) = 20 + 0*Q$

The demand curve represents the home country's demand for a homogeneous good (e.g. corn, iron, rubber, etc.). The domestic supply curve is a typical upward-sloping curve. The world market price is $20; thus, persons may import as much as they want at a constant price of $20. In other words, the world supply curve is perfectly elastic at a price of $20. Assume that an import quota of 4 units is established.

Prepare the following:
a.   Table of Q (from 0 to 10, in increments of 1), P(QD), P(QS-domestic), and P(QS-world).
b.   Graph the domestic demand curve (P(QD), domestic supply curve (P(QS-d), world supply curve (P(QS-w), and a vertical line at the quantity of 4 to illustrate the effect of the quota.
c.   What is equilibrium price and quantity before and after the quota?
d.   Who are the winners and losers from the quota?

59.   ECONOMIC IMPACT OF AN IMPORT QUOTA

Same as previous assignment, except for the following changes:
        1.   The demand equation is as follows: $P(QD) = 120 - 10*Q$
        2.   The world market price is $30.
        3.   The domestic supply and world supply equations are as follows:
                $P(QS\text{-}d) = 20 + 10*Q$
                $P(QS\text{-}w) = 30 + 0*Q$
        4.   The quota is set at 3 units.

60.   ECONOMIC IMPACT OF A TARIFF

Background information for this assignment is on page 89.
Use the following information and analyze the impact of a tariff. Use the following equation

to prepare a domestic demand curve:

$$P(QD) = 120 - 1*Q$$

Use the following equations to prepare a supply curve before and after the tariff is implemented. The tariff is set at $20.

$$P(QS) = 20 + 1*Q$$
$$P(QS)+T = (20 + 1*Q) + T$$

Prepare the following:

a.   Table of Q (from 0 to 100, in increments of 10), P(QD), P(QS), and P(QS)+T.
b.   Graph of the demand curve, P(QD); supply curve before tariff, P(QS); and supply curve after tariff, P(QS)+T.
c.   What is equilibrium price and quantity before and after the tariff?
d.   What is the protective effect and revenue effect of the tariff?

61.   ECONOMIC IMPACT OF A TARIFF

Same as Assignment 60, except the tariff is set at $40 rather than $20.

62.   ECONOMIC IMPACT OF A TARIFF

Same as Assignment 60, except the tariff is set at $60 rather than $20.

63.   STATEMENT OF CASH FLOWS -- INVESTING ACTIVITIES

During fiscal year 20x5, The Home Depot which operates over 400 home improvement centers throughout the United States, reported net income of $604 million and paid $162 million to acquire other businesses. Home Depot paid $1,103 million to open new stores and sold property, plant, and equipment for $50 million. The company purchased long-term investments in stocks and bonds at a cost of $94 million and sold other long-term investments for $454 million. During the year, the company also cashed in other investments for $96 million.

Prepare the investing activities section of The Home Depot's statement of cash flows. Based on The Home Depot's investing activities, does it appear that the company is growing or shrinking? How can you tell?

64. STATEMENT OF CASH FLOWS

The income statement and additional data of Aggieland Computing Company follow:

Aggieland Computing Company
Income Statement
Year Ended September 30, 20x2

Revenues:

Sales revenue....................................		$237,000
Expenses:		
Cost of goods sold.............................	103,000	
Salary expense..................................	45,000	
Depreciation expense..........................	29,000	
Rent expense....................................	11,000	
Interest expense................................	2,000	
Income tax expense............................	9,000	199,000
Net income......................................		$ 38,000

Additional data during fiscal year 20x2:

a. Collections from customers were $7,000 more than sales.

b. Payments to suppliers were $5,000 less than the sum of cost of goods sold plus rent expense.

c. Payment to employees were $1,000 more than salary expense.

d. Interest expense and income tax expense equal their cash amounts.

e. Acquisition of equipment is $116,000. Of this amount, $101,000 was paid in cash, $15,000 by signing a long-term note payable. Aggieland sold no equipment during fiscal year 20x2.

f. Proceeds from sales of land, $14,000.

g. Proceeds from issuance of common stock, $35,000.

h. Payment of long-term note payable, $20,000.

i. Payment of dividends, $10,000.

j. Decrease in cash balance, $4,000.

1. Prepare Aggieland Computing Company's statement of cash flows and accompanying schedule of noncash investing and financing activities. Report operating activities by the **direct** method.

2. Evaluate Aggieland Computing Company's cash flows for the year. In your evaluation, mention all three categories of cash flows (operating, investing, and financing), and give the reason for your evaluation.

65. FINANCIAL RATIOS

Use the following formulas to compute financial ratios for Junior's Computer Store for 20x4. The balance sheet and income statement for 20x4 and 20x3 are provided below. Design the worksheet so that the financial statements are in the input area and the financial ratios are in the output area.

FINANCIAL RATIOS

Liquidity Ratios:

Current Ratio	=	(Cur. Assets)/(Cur. Liabilities)
Acid-Test Ratio	=	(Cur. Assets - Inven. - Prepaid Exp.)/(Cur. Liabilities)

Activity Ratios:

Receivables Turnover	=	(Net Credit Sales)/(Avg. A/R)
Inventory Turnover	=	(Cost of Goods Sold)/(Avg. Inventory)
Asset Turnover	=	(Net Sales)/(Avg. Assets)

Profitability Ratios:

Earnings Per Share	=	(Net Inc. - Pref. Div.)/(Common Shares Outstanding)
Price to Earnings (P/E)	=	(Market Price per Com. Share)/(EPS)
Dividend Payout	=	(Div. per Com. Share)/(EPS)
Sales Profit Margin	=	(Net Income)/(Net Sales)
Return on Assets	=	(Net Income + Int. Exp. - Tax Savings from Int. Exp.)/(Avg. Assets)
Return on Com Stk Equity	=	(Net Inc. - Pref. Div.)/(Avg. Com. Stk Equity)

Financial Stability Ratios:

Total Debt to Total Assets	=	(Total Liabilities)/(Total Assets)
Times Interest Earned	=	(Earnings before Int. and Taxes)/(Interest Charges)
Book Value Per Share	=	(Com. Stk Equity)/(Com. Shares Outstanding)
Cash Flow Per Share	=	(Net Income + Noncash Charges)/(Com. Shares Outstanding)

FINANCIAL STATEMENTS

Junior's Computer Store
Comparative Balance Sheets
12/31/x4 and 12/31/x3

	12/31/x4	12/31/x3
ASSETS:		
Cash	$1,200,000	$ 1,100,000
Accounts Receivable	780,000	550,000
Inventory	1,850,000	1,600,000
Fixed Assets (net)	8,200,000	7,200,000
Total Assets	$12,030,000	$10,450,000
LIABILITIES:		
Accounts Payable	$1,200,000	$900,000
Long-Term Debt	1,730,000	430,000
Total Liabilities	$2,930,000	$1,330,000
STOCKHOLDERS EQUITY:		
Preferred stock, $100 par, 12% cum	$1,800,000	$1,800,000
Common stock, $100 par	7,000,000	7,000,000
Retained Earnings	300,000	320,000
Total	$9,100,000	$9,120,000
Total Liabilities + Stockholders Equity	$12,030,000	$10,450,000
Market Price of Common Stock	$109	$107

Junior's Computer Store
Comparative Income Statements
FYE 12/31/x4 and 12/31/x3

	12/31/x4	12/31/x3
Sales	$4,000,000	$3,300,000
Cost of Goods Sold	2,200,000	1,650,000
Gross Profit	$1,800,000	$1,650,000
Operating Expenses:		
Depreciation	$738,000	$576,000
Advertising	45,000	38,000
Other	120,000	140,000
Total Operating Expense	$903,000	$754,000
Operating Income	$897,000	$896,000
Interest on Long-Term Debt	80,000	80,000
Income Before Taxes	$817,000	$816,000
Taxes	326,800	326,400
Net Income	$490,200	$489,600
Dividends Declared on Preferred Stock	$220,000	$220,000
Dividends on Common Stock	290,200	299,600
Net Income to Retained Earnings	($20,000)	($30,000)

NOTE: All sales are credit sales; the tax rate is 40%.

66.   FINANCIAL RATIOS

Same as the previous assignment but change the following 20x4 items:

A.	Accounts Receivable:	$780,000 to $1,780,000
B.	Accounts Payable:	$1,200,000 to $1,400,000
C.	Retained Earnings:	$300,000 to $1,100,000
D.	Sales:	$4,000,000 to $5,000,000

NOTE: The change in these financial statement items will affect other items.

67.   COMMON-SIZE BALANCE SHEETS

Using the comparative balance sheets in Assignment 65, prepare common-size balance sheets. To prepare common-size balance sheets, divide all items by the "total assets" amount; thus, total assets each year (i.e., 20x4 and 20x3) will be shown as 100 percent.

68.   COMMON-SIZE BALANCE SHEETS

Using the revisions to the 20x4 balance sheet given in Assignment 66, prepare common-size balance sheets for 20x4 and 20x3.

69.   HORIZONTAL ANALYSIS OF INCOME STATEMENTS

Prepare a horizontal analysis of the following comparative income statement of Dynasty International. Round percentage changes to the nearest one-tenth percent (three decimal places):

Dynasty International
Comparative Income Statement
Years Ended December 31, 20x9 and 20x8

	20x9	**20x8**
Total revenue............................	$410,000	$373,000
Expenses:		
Cost of goods sold..................	$202,000	$188,000
Selling and general expenses..	98,000	93,000
Interest expense......................	7,000	4,000
Income tax expense................	42,000	37,000
Total expenses........................	349,000	322,000
Net income................................	$ 61,000	$ 51,000

Why did net income increase by a higher percentage than total revenues during 20x9?

SOLUTIONS

to

Selected Assignments

1.   INCOME STATEMENT

FILE IDENTIFICATION AREA:
Name:
Date Created:
Filename:

INPUT AREA:

Sales: $200,000

OUTPUT AREA:

CHRIS RAY'S CARD SHOP
INCOME STATEMENT
FYE 12/31/x1

Sales	$200,000
Cost of Sales	80,000
Gross profit	$120,000
Operating Expenses	30,000
Net income	$90,000
	======

18.   CASH BUDGET

FILE IDENTIFICATION AREA:
Name:
Date Created:
Filename:

INPUT AREA:

	March	April
Cash Balance, Beginning	$10,000	
Cash Collections	$25,000	$15,000
Sale of Asset	$12,000	$0
Purchases	$12,000	$8,000
Operating Expenses	$5,500	$2,225

OUTPUT AREA:

	March	April
Cash Balance, Beginning	$10,000	$29,500
Cash Collections	$25,000	$15,000
Sale of Asset	$12,000	$0
Total Available	$47,000	$44,500
Cash Disbursements:		
Purchases	$12,000	$8,000
Operating Expenses	$5,500	$2,225
Total Disbursements	$17,500	$10,225
Cash Balance, Ending	$29,500	$34,275

22. BAD DEBT EXPENSE

FILE IDENTIFICATION AREA:
Name:
Date Created:
Filename:

INPUT AREA:

Age of Accounts	A/R Balance	Percent Uncollectible
Under 30 days	$45,000	1%
30-60 days	$25,000	3%
61-120 days	$15,000	10%
Over 120 days	$10,000	30%

OUTPUT AREA:

Bad Debts Expense 20X1:	$5,700
	=======

30. TRACKING INVENTORY QUANTITY

FILE IDENTIFICATION AREA:
Name:
Date Created:
Filename:

INPUT AREA:

Item #	Description	Quantity on hand	Quantity desired
100	HAMMER	8	30
200	SCREWDRIVER	26	20
300	SAW	57	45
400	WRENCH	34	20
500	PLIERS	5	15

OUTPUT AREA:

Item #	Description	Quantity on hand	Quantity desired	Over or (under)
100	HAMMER	8	30	(22)
200	SCREWDRIVER	26	20	6
300	SAW	57	45	12
400	WRENCH	34	20	14
500	PLIERS	5	15	(10)

40.   JOINT COST ALLOCATION

FILE IDENTIFICATION AREA:

Name:
Date Created:
Filename:

INPUT AREA:

Total costs: $600,000

PRODUCT	SALES VALUE AT SPLIT-OFF
A	$800,000
B	$500,000
C	$700,000

OUTPUT AREA:

	A	B	C	TOTAL
Sales value at split-off	$800,000	$500,000	$700,000	$2,000,000
Weights	40.00%	25%	35%	100%
Joint costs allocated	$240,000	$150,000	$210,000	$600,000

44.   WEIGHTED AVERAGE NUMBER OF SHARES OF STOCK

FILE IDENTIFICATION AREA:
Name:
Date Created:
Filename:

INPUT AREA:

JAN - MAR	500
APR - JUL	1200
AUG	1000
SEPT - OCT	1800
NOV	1500
DEC	2000

OUTPUT AREA:

	# of shares	# of months	# of shares * # of months
JAN - MAR	500	3	1,500
APR - JUL	1200	4	4,800
AUG	1000	1	1,000
SEPT - OCT	1800	2	3,600
NOV	1500	1	1,500
DEC	2000	1	2,000
		--------------------	------------------------
		12	14,400

WEIGHTED AVG. NO. OF SHARES O/S FOR YEAR: 1,200
                                                                      ======

50.   INTEREST EARNED

FILE IDENTIFICATION AREA:
Name:
Date Created:
Filename:

INPUT AREA:

Principal	=	$1,000
Interest Rate	=	7.0%
Time Held (Days)	=	61

OUTPUT AREA:

PRINCIPAL	1000
x INTEREST RATE	7.0%
x DAYS HELD/360	61
INTEREST EARNED	$12

53.   FOREIGN CURRENCY TRANSLATION Using Current Rate Method

IDENTIFICATION AREA: Page 1 of 2
Filename:
Designer:
Date:

INPUT AREA:

Adjusted Trial Balance
In Dutch Guilders (DG)
December 31, Year 4

	Debit	Credit
Cash	20,000	
Accounts Receivable	35,000	
Inventory	105,000	
Equipment	60,000	
Accum. Dep.		20,000
Accounts Payable		35,000
Bonds Payable		50,000
Revenues		120,000
General Expenses	108,000	
Depreciation Expense	8,000	
Dividends	4,000	
Common Stock		62,000
Paid-in Capital in Excess of Par		44,000
Retained Earnings		9,000
Total	340,000	340,000

Exchange Rates:

	1 DG = $___
Current Exchange Rate	1.200
Average Exchange Rate	1.250
At July 31, Year 4	1.300
At June 30, Year 1	1.000

Other: All common stock was issued on June 30, Year 1 (i.e., 6/30/Y1).
Dividends were declared and paid on July 31, Year 4.
Translated Retained Earnings at 12/31/Y4 was: $5,500

53.   **Page 2 of 2**

OUTPUT AREA:

Translation from Dutch Guilders to Dollars
Current Rate Method

Debits:		Dutch Guilders	Exchange Rates	U.S. Dollars
	Cash	20,000	1.200	24,000
	A/R	35,000	1.200	42,000
	Inventory	105,000	1.200	126,000
	Fixed Assets	60,000	1.200	72,000
	General Expenses	108,000	1.250	135,000
	Depreciation Exp.	8,000	1.250	10,000
	Dividends (7/31/Y4)	4,000	1.300	5,200
Total		340,000		414,200
Credits:				
	Accum. Depreciation	20,000	1.200	24,000
	A/P	35,000	1.200	42,000
	Bonds Payable	50,000	1.200	60,000
	Revenues	120,000	1.250	150,000
	Common Stock (6/30/Y1)	62,000	1.000	62,000
	Paid-in Cap. (6/30/Y1)	44,000	1.000	44,000
	Retained Earnings	9,000	n.a.	5,500
	Cum. Transl. Adjustment			26,700
Total		340,000		414,200

Index